A book for

My Precious Friend
Rachael

May this little book help guide you

through the big issues of your life.

Lovingly Henrietta

JOHN MACARTHUR

Scriptures to Live By

UNLEASHING GOD'S TRUTH
ONE VERSE AT A TIME

Published by
THOMAS NELSON™
Since 1798

www.thomasnelson.com

Nashville Dallas Mexico City Rio De Janeiro Beijing

Scriptures to Live By
© 2008 by John MacArthur

Published in Nashville, TN, by Thomas Nelson. Thomas Nelson is a trademark of Thomas Nelson, Inc.

Thomas Nelson, Inc., titles may be purchased in bulk for educational, business, fundraising, or sales promotional use. For information, please email SpecialMarkets@ThomasNelson.com.

Published in association with the literary agency of Wolgemuth & Associates, Inc.

Unless otherwise noted, all scripture references are from the *New King James Version of the Bible* ©1979, 1980, 1982, 1992, Thomas Nelson, Inc., Publisher. Used by permission. All rights reserved.

Scripture quotations marked NASB are taken from the *New American Standard Bible.* Copyright © The Lockman Foundation 1960, 1962, 1963, 1968, 1971, 1972, 1973, 1975, 1977, 1995. Used by permission.

"Unleashing God's Truth, One Verse at a Time" is a trademark of Grace to You. All rights reserved.

Designed by the DesignWorks Group

ISBN: 978-14041-0475-4

Printed in China

Contents

Scripture Lights Our Way

*S*criptures to Live By is a starting point for rediscovering the truth about what matters most in life: the truth about who God is, the truth about who we are, and the truth about how God says we should live. These core issues are all clearly addressed throughout the Bible, and understanding them gives you perspective for understanding everything else.

There is great joy in understanding God's Word, and even greater joy in believing it. The Bible is the fountainhead of all spiritual and eternal wisdom and instruction and source of every good thing.

The Bible is the source of *life*. Jesus said, "Man shall not live by bread alone but by every word that proceeds from the mouth of God" (MATTHEW 4:4). God's Word provides life and infuses it with all that makes you want to live it. Once you begin to direct your life according to the Word of God, life in Christ takes on a full, rich, exciting meaning.

The Bible is the source of *power*. As you lift up the Scriptures, you hold in your hands a supernatural resource that has the power to change every area of your life in a way that brings you closer to Christ. It carries the power of conviction (HEBREWS 4:12), the power of salvation (ROMANS 1:16), the power of transformation (ROMANS 12:1-2), and more.

The Bible is the source of *happiness*. True happiness in life results from the transformation of your thinking processes. Colossians 1:16 says that "all things were created through Him and for Him." That includes you. Because you were made for God, you won't know true happiness until you know what pleases Him, and you won't know what that is until you study His manual for living—the Bible. As you learn to live by His principles, you'll begin to experience great satisfaction and happiness. The prophet Jeremiah realized this when he said, "Your words were found, and I ate them, and Your word was to me the joy and rejoicing of my heart" (JEREMIAH 15:16). No matter what your problems may be—relationships, finances, trouble at school or on the job—when you understand what God wants out of your life and all the promises He has prepared for you, it will bring you joy beyond imagining.

The Bible is the source of *ministry*. Paul gave Timothy the strategy for reaching others with the truth when he said, "The things that you have heard from me among many witnesses, commit these to faithful men who will be able to teach others also" (2 TIMOTHY 2:2). Only as you know the Word of God can you pass it on to someone else who can then do the same thing.

The Bible is the source of *truth*. We live in the information age, but what Paul told Timothy two thousand years ago is just as true today: People are "always learning and never able to come to the knowledge of the truth" (2 TIMOTHY 3:7). There's far more information than wisdom.

Real truth—God's truth—changes how you view life, death, time, and eternity. That's because once you are part of God's family, your perspective on life is based on a heavenly viewpoint, not an earthly one. The Bible is the only source of that truth. If you want to know about anything—from God to man, from heaven to earth, from past to future, from the intellect to emotions—it's all in the Bible.

The Bible is the source of *growth*. Every Christian should want to grow in relationship with God—to become more Christlike in character. We want to grow and enjoy the fullness of spiritual life. But that can happen only through daily intake of God's Word. The apostle Peter described the attitude we should have toward our growth through the Bible: "As newborn babes, desire the pure milk of the word, that you may grow thereby" (1 PETER 2:2). Peter did not say "read the Bible" or "study" it or even "meditate on it"; he said *desire* it. That's what Paul called "the love of the truth" (2 THESSALONIANS 2:10). If you seek divine truth as earnestly as some people search after material riches, you will find it, because God has made it available.

Your heavenly Father wants you to grow—by obeying His commands. The Bible is His gift to you as a resource to know those commands. His Word is all you need to obey. I pray that your heart will burn for it.

From *Welcome to the Family*

If you receive my words,
And treasure my commands within you,
So that you incline your ear to wisdom,
And apply your heart to understanding;
Yes, if you cry out for discernment,
And lift up your voice for understanding,
If you seek her as silver,
And search for her as for hidden treasures;
Then you will understand the fear of the LORD,
And find the knowledge of God.
For the LORD gives wisdom;
From His mouth come knowledge and understanding;
He stores up sound wisdom for the upright;
He is a shield to those who walk uprightly;
He guards the paths of justice,
And preserves the way of His saints.
Then you will understand righteousness and justice,
Equity and every good path.

PROVERBS 2:1-9

*I am the LORD, and
there is no other;
There is no God
besides Me.*

ISAIAH 45:5

THE TRUTH ABOUT GOD

God is the ultimate truth in—and beyond—the universe, and before you can have a true understanding of yourself or anything else, you must have a right perspective of God. Let these scriptures guide you into some of the most essential facets of the Almighty.

God is Holy

Exalt the LORD our God,
And worship at His holy hill;
For the LORD our God is holy.

PSALM 99:9

But the LORD of hosts shall be exalted in judgment,
And God who is holy shall be hallowed in righteousness.

ISAIAH 5:16

You alone are holy. For all nations shall come and worship
before You,
For Your judgments have been manifested.

REVELATION 15:4

He who is mighty has done great things for me,
And holy is His name.

LUKE 1:49

I am the LORD your God. You shall therefore consecrate yourselves,
and you shall be holy, for I am holy. Neither shall you defile
yourselves with any creeping thing that creeps on the earth. For
I am the LORD who brings you up out of the land of Egypt, to be
your God. You shall therefore be holy, for I am holy.

LEVITICUS 11:44—45

God is absolutely and perfectly holy (ISAIAH 6:3), therefore He cannot commit or approve of evil (JAMES 1:13). God requires holiness of us as well. First Peter 1:16 admonishes, "Be holy, for I am holy."

As a holy being, He would be perfectly righteous to view all sinners with the utmost contempt. But His is a loving holiness that reaches out to sinners with salvation for them—the antithesis of aloofness or indifference.

Lest we behold His mercy and forget His severity, the prophets repeatedly remind us that ultimately a holy God must wreak vengeance against sin. God is a righteous Judge. For Him to fail to carry out judgment would be inconsistent with His glory, untrue to His Word, and a contradiction of who He is. In other words, the basis for His judgment is His own righteous character. His judgment is as essential to His glory as His love.

From *The God Who Loves*

God is King

For the LORD Most High is awesome;
He is a great King over all the earth.

PSALM 47:2

Jesus answered and said to him, "Most assuredly, I say to you,
unless one is born again, he cannot see the kingdom of God.
. . . Unless one is born of water and the Spirit, he cannot enter
the kingdom of God."

JOHN 3:3, 5

The time is fulfilled, and the kingdom of God is at hand. Repent,
and believe in the gospel.

MARK 1:15

Who is this King of glory?
The LORD of hosts, He is the King of glory!

PSALM 24:10

And the LORD will be king over all the earth. On that day there
will be one LORD—his name alone will be worshiped.

ZECHARIAH 14:9 NLT

He who is the blessed and only Potentate, the King of kings and
Lord of lords.

1 TIMOTHY 6:15

We know God is a king, because the Bible constantly refers to His kingdom—its glory, its preeminence, its inevitability, and its selectivity. We enter the kingdom of God only by the grace of God. There is no place for self–congratulations or human achievement. Remember to thank God for granting you such a gracious salvation.

Few in today's church are as committed to Jesus Christ as the apostle Paul was. Paul exemplifies what Christ was talking about when He said, "If anyone desires to come after Me, let him deny himself, and take up his cross daily, and follow Me" (LUKE 9:23). Paul was so given over to our Lord that he didn't care whether he lived or died. That's an attitude practically unheard of in our materialistic, self–centered, selfish day. Most people today live for everything except what Paul was focused on.

Paul remained joyful as long as his Lord was glorified, even when he was threatened with death. All that mattered to him was that the gospel was advanced, Christ was preached, and the Lord was magnified. The source of his joy was entirely related to the kingdom of God.

From *Truth for Today*

God is Sovereign

I know that whatever God does,
It shall be forever.
Nothing can be added to it,
And nothing taken from it.
God does it, that men should fear before Him.

ECCLESIASTES 3:14

The LORD of hosts has sworn, saying,
"Surely, as I have thought, so it shall come to pass,
And as I have purposed, so it shall stand."

ISAIAH 14:24

I am the LORD, and there is no other;
There is no God besides Me.

ISAIAH 45:5

Now to the King eternal, immortal, invisible, to God who alone
is wise, be honor and glory forever and ever. Amen.

1 TIMOTHY 1:17

I am the Alpha and the Omega, the Beginning and the End, the
First and the Last.

REVELATION 22:13

*S*cripture clearly teaches that God is utterly sovereign over every circumstance, situation, and event:

He controls so-called random happenings. "The lot is cast into the lap, but its every decision is from the Lord" (PROVERBS 16:33).

He is sovereign over the free actions of all moral agents. "The king's heart is in the hand of the LORD . . . He turns it wherever He wishes" (PROVERBS 21:1).

He determines even the most evil acts of sinners. "This Man, delivered up *by the predetermined plan and foreknowledge of God*, you nailed to a cross by the hands of godless men and put Him to death." (ACTS 2:23 NASB, EMPHASIS ADDED).

He appoints the powers that oversee the evil world system. "There is no authority except from God, and those which exist are established by God" (ROMANS 13:1 NASB).

Indeed, the whole course of all events and circumstances is ordained in the divine decree, from the most profound milestone of the divine plan to the most trivial detail. God even determines the number of hairs on our heads (MATTHEW 10:30).

From *The Vanishing Conscience*

God is Unchanging

Forever, O LORD,
Your word is settled in heaven.
Your faithfulness endures to all generations.

PSALM 119:89—90

Of old You laid the foundation of the earth,
And the heavens are the work of Your hands.
They will perish, but You will endure;
. . . You are the same,
And Your years will have no end.

PSALM 102:25—27

Every good gift and every perfect gift is from above, and comes
down from the Father of lights, with whom there is no variation
or shadow of turning.

JAMES 1:17

The counsel of the LORD stands forever,
The plans of His heart to all generations.

PSALM 33:11

He does not retain His anger forever, because He delights in
unchanging love. He will again have compassion on us; He will
tread our iniquities under foot. Yes, Thou wilt cast all their sins
into the depths of the sea.

MICAH 7:18—19 NASB

God Himself says: "I, the Lord, do not change" (MALACHI 3:6 NASB). With God "there is no variation or shadow of turning" (JAMES 1:17). "Jesus Christ is the same the same yesterday, today, and forever" (HEBREWS 13:8).

He is immutable—unchanging. He is not loving one moment and wrathful the next. His wrath coexists with His love; therefore, the two never contradict, even when by human logic they seem in opposition. Such are the perfections of God that we can never begin to comprehend these things. Above all, we must not set aspects of God's nature against one another, as if there were somehow a discrepancy in God. God is always true to Himself and true to His Word (ROMANS 3:4; 2 TIMOTHY 2:13). We can trust that His love and justice truly will remain steadfast forever (PSALM 136).

From *The God Who Loves*

God is Eternal

Your faithfulness endures to all generations;
You established the earth, and it abides.

PSALM 119:90

Before the mountains were brought forth,
Or ever You had formed the earth and the world,
Even from everlasting to everlasting, You are God.

PSALM 90:2

The eternal God is your refuge,
And underneath are the everlasting arms.

DEUTERONOMY 33:27

Now to the King eternal, immortal, invisible, to God who alone
is wise, be honor and glory forever and ever. Amen.

1 TIMOTHY 1:17

Holy, holy, holy,
Lord God Almighty,
Who was and is and is to come!

REVELATION 4:8

God existed before the world began. He had to precede it all because He made it all. God also will continue to exist forever. We know this because He promises to share eternity with us (JOHN 3:16; ROMANS 6:23). Eternity is completely in His command.

Eternal life is the crown that God has promised to those who love Him. It is the believer's ultimate reward. Although we presently experience some of the benefits of eternal life, we possess it on promise; some day we will receive it in its fullness. We are still waiting to enter into our future reward. At the Lord's coming, He will grant to us the fullness of eternal life.

The apostle Paul expressed a similar thought: "Finally, there is laid up for me the crown of righteousness, which the Lord, the righteous Judge, will give to me on that Day, and not to me only but also to all who have loved His appearing" (2 TIMOTHY 4:8). When Christ returns for the church, Christians will be granted a life of eternal righteousness. We will all receive the same crown consisting of the rewards of eternal life, righteousness, and glory.

From *Truth for Today*

God is Omniscient

For His eyes are on the ways of man,
And He sees all his steps.

JOB 34:21

Great is our Lord, and mighty in power;
His understanding is infinite.

PSALM 147:5

But of that day and hour no one knows, not even the angels of
heaven, but My Father only.

MATTHEW 24:36

O LORD, You have searched me and known me.
You know my sitting down and my rising up;
You understand my thought afar off.
You comprehend my path and my lying down,
And are acquainted with all my ways.
For there is not a word on my tongue,
But behold, O LORD, You know it altogether.

PSALM 139:1—4

God knows everything—from the hairs on our heads to the secrets in our hearts. Scripture says, "God withdrew from [King Hezekiah], in order to test him, that He might know all that was in his heart" (2 CHRONICLES 32:31). God didn't need to test Hezekiah to know what was in his heart, because He already knew by omniscience. But He tests us so we can find out. He assists us in doing a spiritual inventory on ourselves by bringing trials into our lives to demonstrate the strength or weakness of our faith.

All the gospel writers made it clear that Jesus knew ahead of time all that would come upon Him. Nothing that night in the Garden of Gethsemane was accidental. Nothing took Him by surprise. He was fully aware of everything that was happening. Nothing was out of His and the Father's omniscient understanding.

This also means that Jesus understood fully all that His dying would entail. He knew in advance about all the pain and agony and taunting and humiliation He would have to bear. Before He ever set foot in that garden, He knew the awful truth about what He would have to endure. But He was nonetheless prepared to submit Himself completely and unreservedly to the Father's will, in order to accomplish the eternal plan of redemption.

From *Truth for Today* and *The Murder of Jesus*

God is Omnipotent

For behold, He who forms mountains,
And creates the wind,
Who declares to man what his thought is,
And makes the morning darkness,
Who treads the high places of the earth—
The LORD God of hosts is His name.

AMOS 4:13

I know that You can do everything,
And that no purpose of Yours can be withheld from You.

JOB 42:2

But Jesus looked at them and said to them, "With men this is
impossible, but with God all things are possible."

MATTHEW 19:26

And I heard, as it were, the voice of a great multitude, as the
sound of many waters and as the sound of mighty thunderings,
saying, "Alleluia! For the Lord God Omnipotent reigns!"

REVELATION 19:6

Keep this commandment without spot, blameless until our Lord
Jesus Christ's appearing, which He will manifest in His own
time, He who is the blessed and only Potentate, the King of
kings and Lord of lords, who alone has immortality, dwelling
in unapproachable light, whom no man has seen or can see, to
whom be honor and everlasting power. Amen.

1 TIMOTHY 6:14—16

Nothing shows God's omnipotence more clearly than His ability to be both fully human and fully divine at His own choosing. In the fullness of time God sent forth His Son, born of a woman. At that very moment, the God of eternity stepped into earthbound time and space. As the apostle John wrote later, "the Word became flesh and dwelt among us" (JOHN 1:14). The omnipotent, omnipresent Lord of the universe appeared as a baby, crying the cry of life, probably weighing less than ten pounds and measuring fewer than twenty–four inches in length. The almighty God used His power to become a helpless human so that He could grow up, die, and then rise again in His full glory.

As the omnipotent Creator and Sovereign of the universe, He demands that finite humans honor Him as such, and it is altogether appropriate that He receive that honor.

From *God in the Manger* and
Introduction to Biblical Counseling

God is Omnipresent

"Am I a God near at hand," says the LORD,
"And not a God afar off?
Can anyone hide himself in secret places,
So I shall not see him?" says the LORD;

JEREMIAH 23:23—24

For where two or three are gathered together in My name, I am there in the midst of them.

MATTHEW 18:20

Where can I go from Your Spirit?
Or where can I flee from Your presence?
If I ascend into heaven, You are there;
If I make my bed in hell, behold, You are there.
If I take the wings of the morning,
And dwell in the uttermost parts of the sea,
Even there Your hand shall lead me,
And Your right hand shall hold me.

PSALM 139:7—12

The eyes of the LORD are in every place,
Keeping watch on the evil and the good.

PROVERBS 15:3

They should seek the Lord, in the hope that they might grope for Him and find Him, though He is not far from each one of us.

ACTS 17:27

*T*he heart of Jewish worship took place in Jerusalem, where God commanded His temple be built. His decrees were very specific about how, when, and where certain rites could be performed, and the most sacred ceremonies occurred in the Most Holy Place behind the temple veil where only the high priest could go. But the heart of the Book of Hebrews focuses on the high priesthood of Jesus. It is a superior priesthood that, more than anything else, makes the New Covenant superior to the Old. He alone has done what all the priests together of the old order did not do and could never have done. In one perfect and final act of sacrifice, He opened the way to God permanently. As a result, anyone at any time, by faith in Christ, now may enter into God's presence.

When Jesus' flesh was torn at His crucifixion, so was the temple veil that symbolically separated men from God's presence (MATTHEW 27:51). When the high priest on the Day of Atonement entered the Most Holy Place, the people waited outside for him to return. When Christ entered the heavenly temple He did not return. Instead, He opened the curtain and exposed the Most Holy Place so that we could follow Him.

God is everywhere. His worship should be everywhere too.

From *MacArthur Bible Studies: Hebrews*

God is the Creator

For thus says the LORD,
Who created the heavens,
Who is God,
Who formed the earth and made it,
Who has established it,
Who did not create it in vain,
Who formed it to be inhabited:
"I am the LORD, and there is no other."

ISAIAH 45:18

I have made the earth, the man and the beast that are on the ground, by My great power and by My outstretched arm, and have given it to whom it seemed proper to Me.

JEREMIAH 27:5

All things were made through Him, and without Him nothing was made that was made.

JOHN 1:3

[Men] exchanged the truth of God for the lie, and worshiped and served the creature rather than the Creator, who is blessed forever. Amen.

ROMANS 1:25

*T*he Bible gives a clear and cogent account of the beginnings of the cosmos and humanity. God created the universe out of *nothing*. He spoke it into existence by His Word. Although the biblical account clashes at many points with naturalistic and evolutionary hypotheses, it is not in conflict with a single scientific fact. The conflict is not between science and Scripture, but between the biblicist's confident faith and the naturalist's willful skepticism.

When the New Testament refers to creation, it always refers to a past, completed event—an immediate work of God, not a still-occurring process of evolution. The promised New Creation, a running theme in both Old and New Testaments, is portrayed as an immediate creation, too—not an eons-long process.

In fact, the model for the New Creation is the original creation (ROMANS 8:21; REVELATION 21:1, 5). Hebrews 11:3 even makes belief in creation by divine fiat the very essence of faith itself: "By faith we understand that the worlds were framed by the word of God, so that the things which are seen were not made of things which are visible." Creation *ex nihilo* (out of nothing) is the clear and consistent teaching of the Bible.

From *Battle for the Beginning*

God is Righteous

For the LORD is righteous,
He loves righteousness;
His countenance beholds the upright.

PSALM 11:7

Let the heavens declare His righteousness,
For God Himself is Judge.

PSALM 50:6

Your righteousness, O God, is very high,
You who have done great things;
O God, who is like You?

PSALM 71:19

Righteousness and justice are the foundation of His throne. . . .
The heavens declare His righteousness,
And all the peoples see His glory.

PSALM 97:2, 6

The LORD is righteous in all His ways,
Gracious in all His works.

PSALM 145:17

If we do not have a growing awe about the holiness of God and His righteous judgment of sin, our understanding of God's grace and mercy will fade away. Without an acknowledgment that God can and does punish, the possibility of mercy and forgiveness carries little weight. If we do not seek to see the entire scope of God's actions and character, we will tend to gravitate to what we like or don't like and miss the connections.

"Do not think in your heart, after the LORD your God has cast them out before you, saying, 'Because of my righteousness the LORD has brought me in to possess this land'; but it is because of the wickedness of these nations that the LORD is driving them out from before you" (DEUTERONOMY 9:4).

How did Jesus fulfill the righteousness of God? By dying on a cross. Whatever Jesus' baptism means, it is somehow connected to the time when God in His righteous indignation poured out vengeance on the Lord Jesus Christ, the perfect sacrifice. All righteousness was then fulfilled, and a righteous God was satisfied and able to impute righteousness to believing people.

From *The MacArthur Quick Reference Guide to the Bible*
and *Rediscovering Pastoral Ministry*

God is Love

The LORD has appeared of old to me, saying:
"Yes, I have loved you with an everlasting love;
Therefore with lovingkindness I have drawn you."

JEREMIAH 31:3

Now hope does not disappoint, because the love of God has been poured out in our hearts by the Holy Spirit who was given to us. . . . God demonstrates His own love toward us, in that while we were still sinners, Christ died for us.

ROMANS 5:5, 8

Beloved, let us love one another, for love is of God; and everyone who loves is born of God and knows God. He who does not love does not know God, for God is love. In this the love of God was manifested toward us, that God has sent His only begotten Son into the world, that we might live through Him. In this is love, not that we loved God, but that He loved us and sent His Son to be the propitiation for our sins. . . . God is love, and he who abides in love abides in God, and God in him. . . . We love Him because He first loved us.

1 JOHN 4:7–12, 16–19

But whoever keeps His word, truly the love of God is perfected in him. By this we know that we are in Him.

1 JOHN 2:5

GOD *is* love. His mercy is over all His works. He manifests His love to all. But the highest expression of His love is manifest to those who by sheer grace He lovingly draws to Himself.

Therefore to those of us who believe, God's love is a uniquely precious reality, albeit an unfathomable one. There is no way we can scale the height of it. There is no way we can imagine the breadth of it or span the width of it. Nevertheless, by God's grace we can know the love of Christ, which passes knowledge (EPHESIANS 3:18–19).

We daily benefit from the goodness of His love. He gives us richly all things to enjoy (1 TIMOTHY 6:17). More than that, His love is shed abroad in our own hearts (ROMANS 5:5). I know of no greater source of comfort, no more sure foundation for our security, no richer source of contentment.

From *The God Who Loves*

God is Gracious

The LORD is righteous in all His ways,
Gracious in all His works.

PSALM 145:17

By grace you have been saved through faith, and that not of
yourselves; it is the gift of God, not of works, lest anyone should
boast.

EPHESIANS 2:8—9

Where sin abounded, grace abounded much more, so that as sin
reigned in death, even so grace might reign through righteousness
to eternal life through Jesus Christ our Lord.

ROMANS 5:20—21

Of His fullness we have all received, and grace for grace. For the
law was given through Moses, but grace and truth came through
Jesus Christ.

JOHN 1:16—17

Ｇod's grace is a spiritual dynamic that works in the lives of the redeemed, "instructing us to deny ungodliness and worldly desires and to live sensibly, righteously and godly in the present age" (TITUS 2:12 NASB). Grace is God presently at work in our lives. By grace "we are His workmanship, created in Christ Jesus for good works, which God prepared beforehand, that we should walk in them" (EPHESIANS 2:10). By grace He "gave Himself for us, that He might redeem us from every lawless deed and purify for Himself a people for His own possession, zealous for good deeds" (TITUS 2:14 NASB).

That ongoing work of grace in the Christian's life is as much a certainty as justification, glorification, or any other aspect of God's redeeming work. "I am confident of this very thing, that He who began a good work in you will perfect it until the day of Christ Jesus" (PHILIPPIANS 1:6 NASB). Salvation is wholly God's work, and He finishes what He starts. His grace *is* sufficient. And it is potent. It cannot be defective in any regard. "Grace" that does not affect one's behavior is not the grace of God.

From *The Gospel According to the Apostles*

God is Just

Shall not the Judge of all the earth do right?

GENESIS 18:25

The Lord is not slack concerning His promise, as some count slackness, but is longsuffering toward us, not willing that any should perish but that all should come to repentance.

2 PETER 3:9

For God is not unjust to forget your work and labor of love which you have shown toward His name, in that you have ministered to the saints, and do minister.

HEBREWS 6:10

With righteousness He shall judge the world,
And the peoples with equity.

PSALM 98:9

And if you call on the Father, who without partiality judges according to each one's work, conduct yourselves throughout the time of your stay here in fear.

1 PETER 1:17

God is a just God. His justice is as unchanging as any other aspect of His character. God cannot change His mind or lower His moral standards. Since He is utterly perfect, any change at all would diminish His perfection—and that would be unthinkable. So His justice is inflexible; His holy nature demands that it be so.

As Creator, He is entitled to rule over all His creatures any way He pleases. The Potter quite simply has power over the clay to fashion it any way He desires. He makes the laws; He determines the standards; and He judges accordingly. He created everything for His own pleasure; and He has every right to do so. He also has total power to determine the principles by which His creation must function.

In short, He has the absolute right to do whatever He determines to do. And because He is righteous, He rules in perfect righteousness, always holding to the highest standard of truth and perfect virtue.

From *The God Who Loves*

God is Merciful

Therefore be merciful, just as your Father also is merciful.

LUKE 6:36

Oh, give thanks to the LORD, for He is good!
For His mercy endures forever.

1 CHRONICLES 16:34

All the paths of the LORD are mercy and truth,
To such as keep His covenant and His testimonies.

PSALM 25:10

You, O Lord, are a God full of compassion, and gracious,
Longsuffering and abundant in mercy and truth.

PSALM 86:15

Righteousness and justice are the foundation of Your throne;
Mercy and truth go before Your face.

PSALM 89:14

The Lord—the Judge Himself—is a stronghold for those who seek refuge in Him by faith. Those words in a nutshell contain the entire gospel of justification by faith. The same God who threatens judgment against the wicked lovingly, compassionately invites sinful souls in despair to find their refuge in Him. He alone will be their haven, their stronghold, their protection from divine judgment. He offers mercy.

How does He shelter those who trust Him? He covers them with His own righteousness, which is theirs by faith (PHILIPPIANS 3:9). That's why in the Old Testament He is called "THE LORD OUR RIGHTEOUSNESS" (JEREMIAH 23:6).

In the New Testament we learn that the very righteousness of God in Christ is imputed to believers—solely by faith and not owing to any works performed by the believing one (ROMANS 4:4–6). In God's mercy He gives us what we cannot earn on our own.

Christ Himself—in His infinite mercy—has already fulfilled the righteous requirements of the law on behalf of believers, and died in their place to pay sin's dreadful price. All believers in Christ are therefore both freed from their guilt and vested with Christ's perfect righteousness. That is the only way sinners can ever find peace with a just, merciful God (ROMANS 5:1).

From *The God Who Loves*

God is Perfect

As for God, His way is perfect.

2 SAMUEL 22:31

Therefore you shall be perfect, just as your Father in heaven is perfect.

MATTHEW 5:48

And do not be conformed to this world, but be transformed by the renewing of your mind, that you may prove what is that good and acceptable and perfect will of God.

ROMANS 12:2

Every good gift and every perfect gift is from above, and comes down from the Father of lights, with whom there is no variation or shadow of turning.

JAMES 1:17

Only the perfect God–Man could bring God and man together. "For there is one God and one Mediator between God and men, the Man Christ Jesus" (1 TIMOTHY 2:5). Christ sets an unattainable standard of perfection, and He demands that we meet that standard (MATTHEW 5:48).

This sums up what the law itself demanded (JAMES 2:10). Though this standard is impossible to meet, God could not lower it without compromising His own perfection. He who is perfect could not set an imperfect standard of righteousness. The marvelous truth of the gospel is that Christ has met this standard on our behalf.

From *The MacArthur Study Bible*

God is Trustworthy

So shall I have an answer for him who reproaches me,
For I trust in Your word. . . .
The entirety of Your word is truth,
And every one of Your righteous judgments endures forever.

PSALM 119:42, 160

Trust in the LORD with all your heart,
And lean not on your own understanding;
In all your ways acknowledge Him,
And He shall direct your paths.

PROVERBS 3:5—6

Those who trust in the LORD are like Mount Zion, which cannot be moved, but abides forever. As the mountains surround Jerusalem, so the LORD surrounds His people from this time forth and forever.

PSALM 125:1—2

Trust in the LORD forever,
For in YAH, the LORD, is everlasting strength.

ISAIAH 26:4

"Faith" (in Greek, *pistis*), means "confident trust in God for everything, an absolute loyalty to the Lord." It is unwavering confidence in God's power, plan, provision, and promise. The man of God lives by faith. He trusts in the sovereign God to keep His word, to meet all his needs, and provide the resources he needs to pursue his ministry. He can say with Paul:

I have learned to be content in whatever circumstances I am. I know how to get along with humble means, and I also know how to live in prosperity; in any and every circumstance I have learned the secret of being filled and going hungry, both of having abundance and suffering need. I can do all things through Him who strengthens me (PHILIPPIANS 4:11–13 NASB).

Paul knew he could trust God to deliver him just as God had delivered Job. He was confident his circumstances would work out for good, whether he was released from prison, vindicated at his trial, and delivered from execution or passed into glory as a martyr. You may not face the same trials as Paul, but whatever your circumstances, the same confident trust is available to you.

From *Truth for Today*

God Is the Father

There is one God, the Father, of whom are all things, and we for Him; and one Lord Jesus Christ, through whom are all things, and through whom we live.

1 CORINTHIANS 8:6

But now, O LORD,
You are our Father;
We are the clay, and You our potter;
And all we are the work of Your hand.

ISAIAH 64:8

For you are all sons of God through faith in Christ Jesus.

GALATIANS 3:26

For as many as are led by the Spirit of God, these are sons of God. For you did not receive the spirit of bondage again to fear, but you received the Spirit of adoption by whom we cry out, "Abba, Father."

ROMANS 8:14—15

While God is the Father of all people in a general sense because He created them (ACTS 17:24–28), only those who have put their faith in Jesus Christ are God's true spiritual children; unbelievers are the children of Satan (1 JOHN 3:10).

Like the father of the prodigal son, God loves us constantly. He forgives eagerly, loves lavishly, and does not deal with us according to our sins, or reward us according to our iniquities (PSALM 103:10). Moreover, He does something the prodigal son's father could not do: He sovereignly draws us to Himself. His love is like a cord that draws us inexorably to Him (HOSEA 11:4). "He chose us in [Christ] before the foundation of the world, that we should be holy and blameless before Him. In love He predestined us to adoption as sons through Jesus Christ to Himself, according to the kind intention of His will" (EPHESIANS 1:4–5 NASB). And "whom He predestined . . . these He also glorified" (ROMANS 8:30 NASB). He sees the process through to the end.

From *The MacArthur Study Bible*
and *The God Who Loves*

God Is the Son

These are written that you may believe that Jesus is the Christ, the Son of God, and that believing you may have life in His name.

JOHN 20:31

For God so loved the world that He gave His only begotten Son, that whoever believes in Him should not perish but have everlasting life. For God did not send His Son into the world to condemn the world, but that the world through Him might be saved.

JOHN 3:16—17

Whoever denies the Son does not have the Father either; he who acknowledges the Son has the Father also.

1 JOHN 2:23

The Holy Spirit descended in bodily form like a dove upon [Jesus], and a voice came from heaven which said, "You are My beloved Son; in You I am well pleased."

LUKE 3:22

*J*esus Christ, the second person of the Trinity, possesses all the divine excellencies, and in these He is co—equal, co-substantial, and co—eternal with the Father (JOHN 10:10; 14:9). God the Father created "the heavens and the earth and all that is in them" according to His own will, through His Son, Jesus Christ, by whom all things continue in existence and in operation (JOHN 1:3; COLOSSIANS 1:15—17; HEBREWS 1:2).

In His Incarnation (God becoming man), Christ surrendered only the prerogatives of deity but nothing of the divine essence, either in degree or kind. In His Incarnation, the eternally existing Second Person of the Trinity accepted all the essential characteristics of humanity and so became the God—Man, deity and humanity in indivisible oneness (MICAH 5:2; JOHN 5:23; 14:9—10; PHILIPPIANS 2:5—8; COLOSSIANS 2:9).

In the Resurrection of Jesus Christ from the grave, God confirmed the deity of His Son and gave proof that God has accepted the atoning work of Christ on the Cross. Jesus' bodily Resurrection is also the guarantee of a future resurrection life for all believers (JOHN 5:26—29; 14:19; ROMANS 4:25; 6:5—10; 1 CORINTHIANS 15:20, 23).

From *MacArthur's Quick Reference Guide to the Bible*

God Is the Holy Spirit

My Spirit who is upon you, and My words which I have put in your mouth, shall not depart from your mouth, nor from the mouth of your descendants.

ISAIAH 59:21

The Spirit also helps in our weaknesses. For we do not know what we should pray for as we ought, but the Spirit Himself makes intercession for us with groanings which cannot be uttered. Now He who searches the hearts knows what the mind of the Spirit is, because He makes intercession for the saints according to the will of God.

ROMANS 8:26—27

I will pray the Father, and He will give you another Helper, that He may abide with you forever—the Spirit of truth, whom the world cannot receive, because it neither sees Him nor knows Him; but you know Him, for He dwells with you and will be in you.

JOHN 14:16—17

Do you not know that you are the temple of God and that the Spirit of God dwells in you?

1 CORINTHIANS 3:16

$\mathcal{J}$esus gave extensive teaching about the Holy Spirit and His role (JOHN 14:16–26). He spoke of the Spirit as a Person, not an influence, not a mystical power, not some ethereal, impersonal, phantom force. The Spirit has all the attributes of personality—mind (ROMANS 8:27), emotions (EPHESIANS 4:30), and will (HEBREWS 2:4)—and all the attributes of deity (ACTS 5:3–4).

After Jesus ascended to heaven, one of the crucial ministries of the Holy Spirit was to bring to the disciples' minds what Jesus had said and to teach them what He meant (JOHN 14:25–26). The Spirit guides us into the truth of God's Word (JOHN 14:17). He teaches us, affirms the truth in our hearts, convicts us of sin, and often brings to mind specific truths and statements of Scripture that are applicable to our lives (1 CORINTHIANS 2:10).

Our Lord also promised that the Holy Spirit would take up permanent, uninterrupted residence within His disciples (JOHN 14:23). Personal rebirth is the Holy Spirit's sovereign work (JOHN 3:8), and every aspect of true spiritual growth in the life of the believer is prompted by the Spirit, using the truth of Scripture (JOHN 17:17). Only the Holy Spirit can work fundamental changes in the human heart.

From *Introduction to Biblical Counseling*

God is Triune

Go therefore and make disciples of all the nations, baptizing them in the name of the Father and of the Son and of the Holy Spirit.

MATTHEW 28:19

The Helper, the Holy Spirit, whom the Father will send in My name, He will teach you all things, and bring to your remembrance all things that I said to you.

JOHN 14:26

The grace of the Lord Jesus Christ, and the love of God, and the communion of the Holy Spirit be with you all. Amen.

2 CORINTHIANS 13:14

Elect according to the foreknowledge of God the Father, in sanctification of the Spirit, for obedience and sprinkling of the blood of Jesus Christ: Grace to you and peace be multiplied.

1 PETER 1:2

For there are three that bear witness in heaven: the Father, the Word, and the Holy Spirit; and these three are one.

1 JOHN 5:7

*I*n Genesis 1:26, for the first time in the Bible, God introduces Himself with personal pronouns. Significantly, they are plural pronouns. Not, "Let *Me* . . ." but, "Let *Us* make man in *Our* image," and thus we are introduced to a plurality of relationships in the Godhead.

The same truth is unfolded with even more clarity in the first chapter of John's Gospel, which begins with an echo of Genesis 1:1: "In the beginning was the Word, and the Word was with God, and the Word was God. He was in the beginning with God. All things were made through Him, and without Him nothing was made that was made" (JOHN 1:1–3). That, of course, refers to the Second Member of the Trinity, Jesus Christ (V. 14)—who was with God at creation and is Himself God.

So, with the light of the New Testament, the plural pronouns of Genesis 1:26 take on a rich depth of meaning . . . All three Members of the Trinity were active in creation. The Father was overseeing and decreeing the work. The eternal Word was "with God" and involved in every aspect of the creative process. And the Spirit was hovering over the waters (GENESIS 1:2), which also suggests the most intimate kind of hands–on involvement in the process.

From *The Battle for the Beginning*

God is Our Friend

And the Scripture was fulfilled which says, "Abraham believed God, and it was accounted to him for righteousness." And he was called the friend of God.

JAMES 2:23

Greater love has no one than this, than to lay down one's life for his friends. You are My friends if you do whatever I command you. No longer do I call you servants, for a servant does not know what his master is doing; but I have called you friends, for all things that I heard from My Father I have made known to you.

JOHN 15:13—15

So the LORD spoke to Moses face to face, as a man speaks to his friend.

EXODUS 33:11

A friend loves at all times,
And a brother is born for adversity.

PROVERBS 17:17

As iron sharpens iron,
So a man sharpens the countenance of his friend.

PROVERBS 27:17

*T*he mark of true love is not unbridled desire or wild passion; it is a giving of oneself. Jesus Himself underscored this when He told His disciples, "Greater love has no one than this, that one lay down his life for his friends" (JOHN 15:13 NASB). If love is a giving of oneself, then the greatest love is shown by laying down one's very life. And of course, such love was perfectly modeled by Christ.

Jesus promised to send His disciples a Friend and Helper exactly like Himself. He had been their Teacher, Leader, and Friend— yet here for the first time, Jesus gave the disciples extensive teaching about the Holy Spirit and His role. Note that our Lord spoke of the Spirit as a Person, not an influence, not a mystical power, not some ethereal, impersonal, phantom force.

There would be, however, a significant change: While Jesus was returning to the Father, the Holy Spirit would "be with you forever." The Holy Spirit is a constant, sure, trustworthy, divine Friend graciously given by Christ to His disciples to be with them forever.

From *The God Who Loves* and
Introduction to Biblical Counseling

We Cannot Fully Understand God

Where is the wise? Where is the scribe? Where is the disputer of this age? Has not God made foolish the wisdom of this world? For since, in the wisdom of God, the world through wisdom did not know God, it pleased God through the foolishness of the message preached to save those who believe. For Jews request a sign, and Greeks seek after wisdom; but we preach Christ crucified, to the Jews a stumbling block and to the Greeks foolishness, but to those who are called, both Jews and Greeks, Christ the power of God and the wisdom of God. Because the foolishness of God is wiser than men, and the weakness of God is stronger than men.

1 CORINTHIANS 1:20—25

For the wisdom of their wise men shall perish,
And the understanding of their prudent men shall be hidden.

ISAIAH 29:14

For since the creation of the world His invisible attributes are clearly seen, being understood by the things that are made, even His eternal power and Godhead, so that they are without excuse, because, although they knew God, they did not glorify Him as God, nor were thankful, but became futile in their thoughts, and their foolish hearts were darkened. Professing to be wise, they became fools, and changed the glory of the incorruptible God into an image made like corruptible man—and birds and four-footed animals and creeping things.

ROMANS 1:18—23

We cannot fully comprehend an infinite God with our finite minds. If we attempt to measure God from a human perspective, all our thinking about Him will be out of whack. And we sin against God when we think things of Him that are unbefitting of His glory.

God Himself rebukes those who underestimate Him by thinking of Him in human terms: "You thought that I was just like you; I will reprove you, and state the case in order before your eyes" (PSALM 50:21 NASB).

Remember how the book of Job ends? God rebuked not only Job's counselors, but also Job himself, for entertaining thoughts about God that were not sufficiently high. Both Job and his counselors were attempting to explain God in human terms. They were appraising God by human standards. They forgot that He is the Potter and we are merely the clay. So God rebuked them.

Job immediately saw his sin: "I have declared that which I did not understand, things too wonderful for me, which I did not know" (JOB 42:3 NASB).

Therefore as we ponder our own difficult questions about God's love, we must take great care lest the very questions themselves provoke us to think inadequate or inappropriate thoughts about God or develop sinful attitudes toward His love and wisdom.

From *The God Who Loves*

God Wants Us to Know Him

God, who at various times and in various ways spoke in time past to the fathers by the prophets, has in these last days spoken to us by His Son.

HEBREWS 1:1—2

I write to you, fathers, because you have known Him who is from the beginning. I write to you, young men, because you have overcome the wicked one. I write to you, little children, because you have known the Father. I have written to you, fathers, because you have known Him who is from the beginning.

1 JOHN 2:13—14

I also count all things loss for the excellence of the knowledge of Christ Jesus my Lord, for whom I have suffered the loss of all things, and count them as rubbish, that I may gain Christ and be found in Him, not having my own righteousness, which is from the law, but that which is through faith in Christ, the righteousness which is from God by faith; that I may know Him and the power of His resurrection, and the fellowship of His sufferings, being conformed to His death.

PHILIPPIANS 3:8—10

I am the LORD your God . . .
And you shall know no God but Me.

HOSEA 13:4

*S*piritual growth progresses from knowing you are a Christian to knowing the Word of God to knowing God Himself. The way to know God is to spend your life focusing on His glory, thus learning to understand the fullness of His person. That focus becomes a magnet drawing you upward through the levels of maturity.

Jesus Christ is the One who introduces men and women to God. Those whom He ushers into the Father's presence all have a loathing of their sin, a desire to be forgiven, and a longing to know God. Those attitudes are the work of God in drawing us to Christ. A response to the gospel message thus begins with a change in attitude toward sin and God.

The more you know God, the more you'll understand who He wants you to be, so the primary pursuit of any believer is to know God (PHILIPPIANS 3:10). That can be achieved only when we study God's character as it is revealed in Scripture.

From *Truth for Today*

God Became a Human

Therefore the Lord Himself will give you a sign: Behold, the virgin shall conceive and bear a Son, and shall call His name Immanuel.

ISAIAH 7:14

And the Word became flesh and dwelt among us, and we beheld His glory, the glory as of the only begotten of the Father, full of grace and truth.

JOHN 1:14

When the fullness of the time had come, God sent forth His Son, born of a woman, born under the law.

GALATIANS 4:4

And the Word became flesh and dwelt among us, and we beheld His glory, the glory as of the only begotten of the Father, full of grace and truth.

JOHN 1:14

For what the law could not do in that it was weak through the flesh, God did by sending His own Son in the likeness of sinful flesh, on account of sin: He condemned sin in the flesh.

ROMANS 8:3

For you know the grace of our Lord Jesus Christ, that though He was rich, yet for your sakes He became poor, that you through His poverty might become rich.

2 CORINTHIANS 8:9

*I*saiah 7:14 says, "The Lord Himself will give you a sign: Behold, a virgin will be with child and bear a son, and she will call His name Immanuel." That virgin's name was Mary.

The name *Immanuel*, however, is the key to this verse—and the heart of the Christmas story. It is a Hebrew name that means literally, "God with us." It is a promise of incarnate deity, a prophecy that God Himself would appear as a human infant, Immanuel, "God with us." This baby who was to be born would be God Himself in human form.

If we could condense all the truths of Christmas into only three words, these would be the words: "God with us." We tend to focus our attention at Christmas on the infancy of Christ. The greater truth of the holiday is His deity. More astonishing than a baby in the manger is the truth that this promised baby is the omnipotent Creator of the heavens and the earth!

From *Truth for Today*

God Sustains Us

These all wait for You,
That You may give them their food in due season.
What You give them they gather in;
You open Your hand, they are filled with good.

PSALM 104:27—28

Are not two sparrows sold for a copper coin? And not one of them
falls to the ground apart from your Father's will. But the very
hairs of your head are all numbered.

MATTHEW 10:29—30

Both riches and honor come from You,
And You reign over all.
In Your hand is power and might;
In Your hand it is to make great
And to give strength to all.

1 CHRONICLES 29:12

In all your ways acknowledge Him,
And He shall direct your paths.

PROVERBS 3:6

*T*rusting Christ means placing oneself in His custody for both life and death. It means we rely on His counsel, trust in His goodness, and entrust ourselves for time and eternity to His guardianship. Real faith, saving faith, is all of me (mind, emotions, and will) embracing all of Him (Savior, Advocate, Provider, Sustainer, Counselor, and Lord God).

Christians are "kept by the power of God through faith" (1 PETER 1:5). Instead of giving them doses of sympathy and commiseration, Peter pointed them to their absolute security as believers. He knew they might be losing all their earthly possessions and even their lives, but he wanted them to know they would never lose what they had in Christ. Their heavenly inheritance was guaranteed. They were being kept by divine power. Their faith would endure through anything. They would persevere through their trials and be found worthy at the end. Their love for Christ would remain intact. Even now, in the midst of their difficulties, God would provide the spiritual deliverance they needed, according to His eternal plan. Those assurances sum up how God sustains every Christian through perseverance.

From *The Gospel According to the Apostles*

God Comforts Us

"Comfort, yes, comfort My people!"
Says your God.

ISAIAH 40:1

Blessed be the God and Father of our Lord Jesus Christ, the Father of mercies and God of all comfort, who comforts us in all our tribulation, that we may be able to comfort those who are in any trouble, with the comfort with which we ourselves are comforted by God.

2 CORINTHIANS 1:3—4

I, even I, am He who comforts you.

ISAIAH 51:12

As one whom his mother comforts,
So I will comfort you;
And you shall be comforted in Jerusalem.

ISAIAH 66:13

God is the ultimate source of every true act of comfort. The Greek word for "comfort" is related to the word *paraclete*, "one who comes alongside to help," which is another name for the Holy Spirit. "Comfort" often connotes softness and ease, but that is not its meaning here. Paul was saying that God came to him in the middle of his sufferings and troubles to strengthen him and give him courage and boldness.

The Holy Spirit, also called the Comforter, encourages persecuted believers to "be patient, brethren, until the coming of the Lord. See *how* the farmer waits for the precious fruit of the earth, waiting patiently for it until it receives the early and latter rain. You also be patient. Establish your hearts, for the coming of the Lord is at hand" (JAMES 5:7—8).

I'm sure the dear saints to whom James was writing longed for God's comfort and justice against their persecutors; but God wanted them to cultivate patience, strength of heart, and a joyful anticipation of Christ's return. Those are far greater benefits than immediate relief from the difficulties and injustices they faced. God would vindicate them, but in His own time.

From *The MacArthur Study Bible*
and *Our Sufficiency in Christ*

God Protects Us

The LORD is my rock and my fortress and my deliverer;
My God, my strength, in whom I will trust.

PSALM 18:2

The Lord will deliver me from every evil work and preserve me
for His heavenly kingdom.

2 TIMOTHY 4:18

The LORD shall preserve your going out and your coming in from
this time forth, and even forevermore.

PSALM 121:8

Fear not, for I am with you;
Be not dismayed, for I am your God.
I will strengthen you,
Yes, I will help you,
I will uphold you with My righteous right hand.

ISAIAH 41:10

Because you have kept My command to persevere, I also will
keep you from the hour of trial which shall come upon the whole
world, to test those who dwell on the earth.

REVELATION 3:10

*M*any Christians are confident that God is able to guard their inheritance but doubt He can guard *them*. They fear they will somehow lose their salvation and forfeit God's promises. That's a popular view but it overlooks the fact that God protects more than our inheritance—He protects *us* as well! Remember, Peter said we "are kept by the power of God through faith for salvation ready to be revealed in the last time" (1 PETER 1:5).

The word translated "protected" is a military term that speaks of a guard. Peter used the present tense to indicate that we are continually under guard. Implied is the idea that we need ongoing protection because we're in a constant battle with Satan and his forces.

We are protected by God's power *through faith*. Faith is God's gift to us; we don't generate it on our own (EPHESIANS 2:8—9; PHILIPPIANS 1:29). Faith is aroused by grace, upheld by grace, and energized by grace. Grace reaches into the soul of the believer, generating and maintaining faith. By God's grace alone we trust Christ, and by grace we continue to believe.

From *Our Sufficiency in Christ*

God Guides Us

However, when He, the Spirit of truth, has come, He will guide you into all truth; for He will not speak on His own authority, but whatever He hears He will speak; and He will tell you things to come.

JOHN 16:13

And the LORD went before them by day in a pillar of cloud to lead the way, and by night in a pillar of fire to give them light, so as to go by day and night. He did not take away the pillar of cloud by day or the pillar of fire by night from before the people.

EXODUS 13:21—22

To give light to those who sit in darkness and the shadow of death, To guide our feet into the way of peace.

LUKE 1:79

However, when He, the Spirit of truth, has come, He will guide you into all truth; for He will not speak on His own authority, but whatever He hears He will speak; and He will tell you things to come.

JOHN 16:13

*I*n John 14:26 Jesus tells His disciples: "But the Helper, the Holy Spirit, whom the Father will send in My name, He will teach you all things."

True, this promise was primarily for the disciples themselves. The Holy Spirit did come to guide and empower them as they wrote inspired Scripture. But Jesus' promise of the Holy Spirit extends to every believer in every age. God plants the Holy Spirit in your life, and then He guides you into more and more truth.

But that's not all. God also provides the textbook for learning truth. In John 17:17 Jesus prayed for His disciples and said: "Sanctify them by Your truth. Your word is truth." And where is God's Word? It's in the Scriptures.

The apostle Paul knew the Holy Spirit as his indwelling teacher, interceder, guide, source of power, and all–sufficient provider. That's what the Spirit is for all believers. Paul's confidence in knowing that all things work together for good (ROMANS 8:28) was based on the provision of the Spirit, who "helps in our weaknesses."

From *Unleashing God's Word in Your Life*
and *Truth for Today*

God Teaches Us

Out of heaven He let you hear His voice, that He might instruct you; on earth He showed you His great fire, and you heard His words out of the midst of the fire.

DEUTERONOMY 4:36

I will instruct you and teach you in the way you should go.

PSALM 32:8

For He instructs him in right judgment, His God teaches him.

ISAIAH 28:26

And they have turned to Me the back, and not the face; though I taught them, rising up early and teaching them, yet they have not listened to receive instruction.

JEREMIAH 32:33

But concerning brotherly love you have no need that I should write to you, for you yourselves are taught by God to love one another.

1 THESSALONIANS 4:9

As the Holy Spirit reveals true wisdom, three elements are discernible: revelation, inspiration, and illumination.

Revelation means the disclosure of something that has been previously hidden, the unveiling of something that has been veiled. The Holy Spirit is the agent who reveals God's wisdom to the Christian as He "searches all things, yes, the deep things of God" (1 CORINTHIANS 2:10).

Inspiration is the method by which the Spirit delivers God's revelation. Paul goes on to say that "we [the apostles] have received, not the spirit of the world, but the Spirit who is from God, that we might know the things that have been freely given to us by God" (1 CORINTHIANS 2:12).

Perhaps the Holy Spirit's most important work is in the third step—*illumination*. Many people have a Bible, but don't really know what's in it. Or they believe in strange and interesting doctrines that are not taught by the Bible at all. The safeguard against misuse of the Bible is the illumination from the Holy Spirit. That is what Paul is talking about when he writes in 1 Corinthians 2:14: "But the natural man does not receive the things of the Spirit of God, for they are foolishness to him; nor can he know them, because they are spiritually discerned."

From *Unleashing God's Word in Your Life*

God Never Does Anything Evil

Let no one say when he is tempted, "I am tempted by God"; for God cannot be tempted by evil, nor does He Himself tempt anyone. But each one is tempted when he is drawn away by his own desires and enticed. Then, when desire has conceived, it gives birth to sin; and sin, when it is full–grown, brings forth death.

JAMES 1:13—15

God is light and in Him is no darkness at all.

1 JOHN 1:5

God is not the author of confusion but of peace.

1 CORINTHIANS 14:33

Through one man sin entered the world, and death through sin, and thus death spread to all men, because all sinned.

ROMANS 5:12

When God finished His creation, He saw everything and declared it "very good" (GENESIS 1:31), and He did not add anything evil to His creation. God may devise calamity as a judgment for the wicked (ISAIAH 45:6–7), but in no sense is He the author of evil.

Instead, all evil in the universe emanates from the sins of fallen creatures. Death, pain, disease, stress, exhaustion, calamity, and all the bad things that happen came as a result of the entrance of sin into the universe (GENESIS 3:14–24). All those evil effects of sin continue to work in the world and will be with us as long as sin is.

God is sovereign over evil, but He is never its author. He simply permits evil agents to work, then overrules evil for His own wise and holy ends. Ultimately He is able to make all things—including all the fruits of all the evil of all time—work together for a greater good (ROMANS 8:28).

From *www.gty.org*

God's Enemy Satan is Real

The great dragon was cast out, that serpent of old, called the Devil and Satan, who deceives the whole world; he was cast to the earth, and his angels were cast out with him.

REVELATION 12:9

Be sober, be vigilant; because your adversary the devil walks about like a roaring lion, seeking whom he may devour.

1 PETER 5:8

You are of your father the devil, and the desires of your father you want to do. He was a murderer from the beginning, and does not stand in the truth, because there is no truth in him. When he speaks a lie, he speaks from his own resources, for he is a liar and the father of it.

JOHN 8:44

There was a day when the sons of God came to present themselves before the LORD, and Satan also came among them.

JOB 1:6

He who sins is of the devil, for the devil has sinned from the beginning. For this purpose the Son of God was manifested, that He might destroy the works of the devil.

1 JOHN 3:8

The name *Satan* is a transliteration of the Hebrew word for "adversary." In its Old Testament occurrences, the word is often used with a definite article, suggesting that it was not originally a proper name but a descriptive expression ("the adversary").

The technical meaning of the Hebrew term conveys a legal nuance that speaks of one's adversary—the one who brings an accusation—in a legal context. And of course, this is perfectly descriptive of Satan's role. He is the accuser of the brethren (REVELATION 12:10). In the Old Testament Book of Job we see him working behind the scenes to discredit and ruin Job. And in the New Testament, he seeks power over Peter, so that he can sift him like wheat at the hour of Peter's greatest vulnerability (LUKE 22:31).

Jesus Himself alluded to Satan as real and historical when He referred to the devil as a murderer and a liar and the father of lying (JOHN 8:44).

From *The Battle for the Beginning*

*Forever, O L*ORD*,*
Your word is
settled in heaven.

PSALM 119:89

THE TRUTH ABOUT SCRIPTURE

If we want to know God, we must read His Word. It's the divine unfolding of the nature and will of God. It's the nourishment that helps us grow in knowledge and love. It's the light to guide us through dark times and the revelation of praise when we worship our Lord. It's the wise companion to aid us in every moment in our lives.

Scripture is God's Inspired Word

All Scripture is given by inspiration of God, and is profitable for doctrine, for reproof, for correction, for instruction in righteousness, that the man of God may be complete, thoroughly equipped for every good work.

2 TIMOTHY 3:16—17

The word of God is living and powerful, and sharper than any two-edged sword, piercing even to the division of soul and spirit, and of joints and marrow, and is a discerner of the thoughts and intents of the heart.

HEBREWS 4:12

Till heaven and earth pass away, one jot or one tittle will by no means pass from the law till all is fulfilled.

MATTHEW 5:18

No prophecy of Scripture is of any private interpretation, for prophecy never came by the will of man, but holy men of God spoke as they were moved by the Holy Spirit.

2 PETER 1:20—21

*T*he Bible is God's written revelation to man (1 CORINTHIANS 2:7–14). It is an objective, propositional revelation (1 THESSALONIANS 2:13), verbally inspired in every word, absolutely inerrant in the original documents, infallible, and God-breathed. The Bible constitutes the only infallible rule of faith and practice (MATTHEW 5:18; 24:35; JOHN 10:35; 16:12–3; 17:17; 1 CORINTHIANS 2:13; 2 TIMOTHY 3:15–17; HEBREWS 4:12).

God spoke in His written Word by a process of dual authorship. The Holy Spirit so superintended the human authors that, through their individual personalities and different styles of writing, they composed and recorded God's Word to man without error in the whole or in the part.

Scripture needs no updating, editing, or refining. Whatever time or culture you live in, it is eternally relevant. It needs no help in that regard. It is pure, sinless, inerrant truth; it is enduring. It is God's revelation for every generation. It was written by the omniscient Spirit of God, who is infinitely more sophisticated than anyone who dares stand in judgment on Scripture's relevancy for our society, and infinitely wiser than all the best philosophers, analysts, and psychologists who pass like a childhood parade into irrelevancy.

From *The MacArthur Study Bible* and
Our Sufficiency in Christ

Scripture Reveals One Glorious Pattern

God, who at various times and in various ways spoke in time past to the fathers by the prophets, has in these last days spoken to us by His Son, whom He has appointed heir of all things, through whom also He made the worlds.

HEBREWS 1:1—2

The law of the LORD is perfect, converting the soul;
The testimony of the LORD is sure, making wise the simple;
The statutes of the LORD are right, rejoicing the heart;
The commandment of the LORD is pure, enlightening the eyes.

PSALM 19:7—8

Forever, O LORD,
Your word is settled in heaven.

PSALM 119:89

*T*he one constant theme unfolding throughout the whole Bible is this: God for His own glory has chosen to create and gather to Himself a group of people to be the subjects of His eternal kingdom; to praise, honor, and serve Him forever; and through whom He will display His wisdom, power, mercy, grace, and glory. To gather His chosen ones, God must redeem them from sin. The Bible reveals God's plan for this redemption from its inception in eternity past to its fulfillment in eternity future. Covenants, promises, and epochs are all secondary to the one continuous plan of redemption.

The Bible is one continuous story of God redeeming His chosen people for the praise of His glory. As God's redemptive purpose and plan unfolds in Scripture, five recurring motifs are constantly emphasized:

1. the nature of God
2. the curse for sin and disobedience
3. the blessing for faith and obedience
4. the Lord Savior and the sacrifice for sin
5. the coming kingdom and glory

Everything fits into this glorious pattern. As you read the Bible, hang the truth on these five hooks, and the Bible will unfold, not as sixty-six separate documents or even two separate testaments but as one book, by one divine Author, who wrote it all with one overarching theme.

From *Unleashing God's Word in Your Life*

Scripture is the Source of Essential Truth

Therefore let him who thinks he stands take heed lest he fall. No temptation has overtaken you except such as is common to man; but God is faithful, who will not allow you to be tempted beyond what you are able, but with the temptation will also make the way of escape, that you may be able to bear it.

1 CORINTHIANS 10:12—13

The word of God is living and powerful, and sharper than any two-edged sword, piercing even to the division of soul and spirit, and of joints and marrow, and is a discerner of the thoughts and intents of the heart.

HEBREWS 4:12

The law of the LORD is perfect, converting the soul;
The testimony of the LORD is sure, making wise the simple;
The statutes of the LORD are right, rejoicing the heart;
The commandment of the LORD is pure, enlightening the eyes;
The fear of the LORD is clean, enduring forever;
The judgments of the LORD are true and righteous altogether.

PSALM 19:7—9

*S*cripture is superior to human wisdom and a more effective discerner of the human heart than any earthly means. The people of God cannot find essential spiritual truth in any resource besides God's Word. Psalm 19 offers a brief, potent statement of the utter sufficiency of the Bible. The first six verses deal with God's revelation of Himself as seen in creation. Verses 7 to 9 describe special revelation, or God's revelation of Himself in His Word. It is this part of the psalm we want to consider most carefully.

- It lists six titles for Scripture: law, testimony, precepts, commandment, fear, and judgments.

- It lists six characteristics of Scripture: It is perfect, it is sure, it is right, it is clear, it is clean, it is true.

- It lists six benefits of Scripture: It restores the soul, it makes wise the simple, it rejoices the heart, it enlightens the eyes, it endures forever, and it is righteous altogether.

- It includes six occurrences of the covenant name of YHWH translated in the phrase "of the Lord," thus reminding us that the source of special revelation is from God.

These verses show the utter comprehensiveness of biblical sufficiency; they are God's own witness and testimony to the total adequacy of His Word for all spiritual needs.

From *Introduction to Biblical Counseling*

Scripture Requires the Holy Spirit for Understanding

These things we also speak, not in words which man's wisdom teaches but which the Holy Spirit teaches, comparing spiritual things with spiritual. But the natural man does not receive the things of the Spirit of God, for they are foolishness to him; nor can he know them, because they are spiritually discerned. But he who is spiritual judges all things, yet he himself is rightly judged by no one. For "who has known the mind of the LORD that he may instruct Him?" But we have the mind of Christ.

1 CORINTHIANS 2:13–16

Give me understanding, and I shall keep Your law;
Indeed, I shall observe it with my whole heart.

PSALM 119:34

He opened their understanding, that they might comprehend the Scriptures.

LUKE 24:45

*T*he Spirit of God revealed God's truth to us not in the words that human wisdom teaches but in words the Holy Spirit teaches. And because we have the Word of God through the Holy Spirit, we can judge, appraise, evaluate all things. Why? Because through the Scriptures and the Spirit we have been given the mind of Christ.

God's Word is living and powerful. It reveals the deepest part of a person's inner soul, "piercing as far as the division of soul and spirit, of both joints and marrow, and able to judge the thoughts and intentions of the heart" (HEBREWS 4:12 NASB). Scripture cuts to the very depth of the deepest part of a person's being so that "all things are open and laid bare" (V. 13 NASB). The Word can do what no psychotherapy can do: it opens the soul.

Although God has graciously supplied pastors and Bible teachers for the edification of the Church, we don't need teachers of mere human wisdom (1 JOHN 2:27). We who have the Holy Spirit living in us have the ability to comprehend eternal truth. Jesus prayed for His disciples, "Sanctify them by Your truth. Your word is truth" (JOHN 17:17). That is as clear a statement as any in all Scripture that sanctification in its fullest sense is accomplished by God's Word.

From *Introduction to Biblical Counseling*

Scripture Reveals the Character of God

Thus says the LORD, your Redeemer,
The Holy One of Israel:
"I am the LORD your God,
Who teaches you to profit,
Who leads you by the way you should go.
Oh, that you had heeded My commandments!
Then your peace would have been like a river,
And your righteousness like the waves of the sea."

ISAIAH 48:17—18

And now, O Lord GOD, You are God, and Your words are true,
and You have promised this goodness to Your servant.

2 SAMUEL 7:28

The words of the LORD are pure words,
Like silver tried in a furnace of earth,
Purified seven times.

PSALM 12:6

For You are my lamp, O LORD;
The LORD shall enlighten my darkness.

2 SAMUEL 22:29

Blessed be the LORD, who has given rest to His people Israel, according
to all that He promised. There has not failed one word of all His
good promise, which He promised through His servant Moses.

1 KINGS 8:56

*A*bove all else, Scripture is God's self-revelation. He reveals Himself as the Sovereign God of the universe who has chosen to make man and to make Himself known to man. In that self-revelation is established His standard of absolute holiness. From Adam and Eve through Cain and Abel and to everyone before and after the law of Moses, the standard of righteousness was established and is sustained to the last page of the New Testament. Violation of it produces judgment, temporal and eternal.

In the Old Testament record, God revealed Himself by the following means: (1) creation, primarily through man, who was made in God's image; (2) angels; (3) signs, wonders, and miracles; (4) visions; (5) the words spoken by prophets and others; (6) written Scripture of the Old Testament.

In the New Testament record, God revealed Himself again by the same means, but more clearly and fully through: (1) creation, through the God-Man, Jesus Christ, who was the very image of God; (2) angels; (3) signs, wonders, and miracles; (4) visions; (5) spoken words by apostles and prophets; (6) the written Scripture of the New Testament.

From *Unleashing God's Word in Your Life*

Scripture Reveals Divine Judgment for Sin

He who despises the word will be destroyed,
But he who fears the commandment will be rewarded.

PROVERBS 13:13

Lay aside all filthiness and overflow of wickedness, and receive
with meekness the implanted word, which is able to save your
souls. But be doers of the word, and not hearers only, deceiving
yourselves.

JAMES 1:21—22

It is good for me that I have been afflicted,
That I may learn Your statutes.

PSALM 119:71

*S*cripture repeatedly deals with the matter of man's sin, which leads to divine judgment. Account after account in Scripture demonstrates the deadly effects in time and eternity of violating God's standard. There are 1,189 chapters in the Bible. Only four of them don't involve a fallen world: the first two and the last two—before the Fall and after the creation of the new heaven and new earth. The rest is a chronicle of the tragedy of sin.

In the Old Testament, God showed the disaster of sin, the relentless record of continual devastation produced by sin and disobedience to God's law.

In the New Testament, the tragedy of sin becomes more clear. The preaching and teaching of Jesus and the apostles begin and end with a call to repentance. King Herod, the Jewish leaders, and the nation of Israel—along with Pilate, Rome, and the rest of the world—all reject the Lord Savior, spurn the truth of God, and thus condemn themselves. The chronicle of sin continues unabated to the end of the age and the return of Christ in judgment. In the New Testament, disobedience is even more flagrant because it involves the rejection of the Lord Savior Jesus Christ in the brighter light of fulfilled truth.

Ultimately, the punishment for sin—man's choice to separate himself from God in this life—is eternal separation from God in the next life.

From *Unleashing God's Word in Your Life*

Scripture Reveals Blessings for Obedience

Most assuredly, I say to you, he who hears My word and believes in Him who sent Me has everlasting life, and shall not come into judgment, but has passed from death into life.

JOHN 5:24

Whoever keeps His word, truly the love of God is perfected in him. By this we know that we are in Him.

1 JOHN 2:5

This Book of the Law shall not depart from your mouth, but you shall meditate in it day and night, that you may observe to do according to all that is written in it. For then you will make your way prosperous, and then you will have good success.

JOSHUA 1:8

Your testimonies are wonderful;
Therefore my soul keeps them.
The entrance of Your words gives light;
It gives understanding to the simple.

PSALM 119:129–130

Keep my commands and live,
And my law as the apple of your eye.
Bind them on your fingers;
Write them on the tablet of your heart.

PROVERBS 7:2–3

Scripture repeatedly promises wonderful rewards in time and eternity to people who trust God and seek to obey Him. In the Old Testament, God showed the blessedness of repentance from sin, faith in Himself, and obedience to His Word—from Abel, through the patriarchs, to the remnant in Israel—and even to the Gentiles who believed (such as the people of Nineveh).

God's standard for man, His will, and His moral law were always made known. To those who faced their inability to keep God's standard, recognized their sin, confessed their impotence to please God by their own effort and works, and asked Him for forgiveness and grace—there came merciful redemption and blessing for time and eternity.

In the New Testament, God again showed the full blessedness of redemption from sin for repentant people. There were those who responded to the preaching of repentance by John the Baptist. Others repented at the preaching of Jesus. Still other Jews obeyed the gospel through the apostles' preaching. And finally, there were Gentiles all over the Roman Empire who believed the gospel. To all those and to all who will believe through all of history, there is blessing promised in this world and the world to come.

From *Unleashing God's Word in Your Life*

Scripture Reveals Jesus and His Sacrifice

[Apollos] vigorously refuted the Jews publicly, showing from the Scriptures that Jesus is the Christ.

ACTS 18:28

Heaven and earth will pass away, but My words will by no means pass away.

MATTHEW 24:35

We have the prophetic word confirmed, which you do well to heed as a light that shines in a dark place, until the day dawns and the morning star rises in your hearts.

2 PETER 1:19

Faith comes by hearing, and hearing by the word of God.

ROMANS 10:17

We speak the wisdom of God in a mystery, the hidden wisdom which God ordained before the ages for our glory, which none of the rulers of this age knew; for had they known, they would not have crucified the Lord of glory.
But as it is written:
"Eye has not seen, nor ear heard,
Nor have entered into the heart of man
The things which God has prepared for those who love Him."
But God has revealed them to us through His Spirit. For the Spirit searches all things, yes, the deep things of God.

1 CORINTHIANS 2:7—10

*J*esus as Savior is the heart of both the Old Testament, which Jesus said spoke of Him in type and prophecy, and the New Testament, which gives the biblical record of His coming.

Salvation is always by the same gracious means, whether during Old or New Testament times. When any sinner comes to God, repentant and convinced he has no power to save himself from the deserved judgment of God, and pleads for mercy through Jesus, God's promise of forgiveness is granted. God then declares him righteous because the sacrifice and obedience of Christ is put to his account. In the Old Testament, God justified sinners that same way, in anticipation of Christ's atoning work. There is, therefore, a continuity of grace and salvation through all of redemptive history. Various covenants, promises, and epochs do not alter that fundamental continuity; neither does the discontinuity between the Old Testament witness (the nation of Israel) and the New Testament witness (the church).

Everything in Scripture points to the Cross. Throughout the Old Testament, the Savior and His sacrifice are promised (GENESIS 3:15; ZECHARIAH 12:10; ISAIAH 53:3–4, 11). In the New Testament, the Lord Savior came and actually provided the promised sacrifice for sin on the Cross.

From *Unleashing God's Word in Your Life*

Scripture Reveals God's Glory and Kingdom

Your kingdom is an everlasting kingdom,
And Your dominion endures throughout all generations.

PSALM 145:13

He remembers His covenant forever,
The word which He commanded, for a thousand generations.

PSALM 105:8—9

Therefore thus says the LORD God of hosts:
"Because you speak this word,
Behold, I will make My words in your mouth fire,
And this people wood,
And it shall devour them."

JEREMIAH 5:14

The grass withers, the flower fades,
But the word of our God stands forever.

ISAIAH 40:8

Scripture brings the whole story of mankind to its God-ordained consummation. Redemptive history is controlled by God, so as to culminate in His eternal glory. The Bible notes several specific features of the end planned by God.

In the Old Testament, there is repeated mention of an earthly kingdom ruled by the Messiah, Lord Savior, who will come to reign. Associated with that kingdom will be the salvation of Israel, the salvation of the Gentiles, the renewal of the earth from the effects of the curse, and the bodily resurrection of God's people who have died. Finally, the Old Testament predicts the creation of a new heaven and a new earth for the godly and a final hell for the ungodly.

In the New Testament, these features are clarified and expanded. The King was rejected and executed, but He promised to come back in glory, bringing judgment, resurrection, and His kingdom for all who believe. Innumerable Gentiles from every nation will be included among the redeemed. Israel will be saved, grafted back into the root of blessing from which she has been temporarily excised. Israel's promised kingdom will be enjoyed, with the Lord Savior reigning on the throne, in the renewed earth, exercising power over the whole world, having taken back His rightful authority and receiving due honor and worship.

From *Unleashing God's Word in Your Life*

We Can Know Scripture is True

I neither received [the Word] from man, nor was I taught it, but it came through the revelation of Jesus Christ.

GALATIANS 1:12

The statutes of the LORD are right, rejoicing the heart;
The commandment of the LORD is pure, enlightening the eyes.

PSALM 19:8

For assuredly, I say to you, till heaven and earth pass away, one jot or one tittle will by no means pass from the law till all is fulfilled.

MATTHEW 5:18

"The word of the LORD endures forever."
Now this is the word which by the gospel was preached to you.

1 PETER 1:25

You know in all your hearts and in all your souls that not one thing has failed of all the good things which the LORD your God spoke concerning you. All have come to pass for you; not one word of them has failed.

JOSHUA 23:14

But the word is very near you, in your mouth and in your heart, that you may do it.

DEUTERONOMY 30:14

The grass withers, the flower fades,
But the word of our God stands forever.

ISAIAH 40:8

*T*here are many evidences of the Bible's truthfulness. Some of them are subjective. For example, I know the Bible is true because of the way its truth has utterly transformed me. My thinking, my desires, and my behavior are all different. One of the Bible's promises is that God will forgive my sins (1 JOHN 1:9). Along with the promise of forgiveness itself, He has given me an amazing sense of peace and freedom from the guilt that once kept me in bondage. So my own experience with the Bible teaches me it is completely trustworthy.

Other proofs of the Bible's reliability are more objective. For instance, archaeology repeatedly and consistently has demonstrated that Scripture is accurate in its descriptions of the ancient world. For example, critics of Scripture doubted the Bible's description of King Solomon's wealth until one of Solomon's chariot cities was unearthed. Additional examples of how archaeology confirms the authority of the Bible could fill dozens of books.

But perhaps the strongest objective argument for the validity of Scripture comes from fulfilled Bible prophecy. Biblical prophecy declares the events of the future with accuracy, which is beyond the capability of human wisdom or anticipation. Despite astronomical odds, hundreds of biblical prophecies have come true, and they make the most objective argument for the Bible's authority.

From *Unleashing God's Word in Your Life*

Scripture is Our Weapon Against Satan

Put on the whole armor of God, that you may be able to stand against the wiles of the devil. For we do not wrestle against flesh and blood, but against principalities, against powers, against the rulers of the darkness of this age, against spiritual hosts of wickedness in the heavenly places. Therefore take up the whole armor of God, that you may be able to withstand in the evil day, and having done all, to stand. . . . And take the helmet of salvation, and the sword of the Spirit, which is the word of God.

EPHESIANS 6:11–13, 17

The word of God is living and powerful, and sharper than any two-edged sword, piercing even to the division of soul and spirit, and of joints and marrow, and is a discerner of the thoughts and intents of the heart.

HEBREWS 4:12

"Is not My word like a fire?" says the LORD,
"And like a hammer that breaks the rock in pieces?"

JEREMIAH 23:29

I am not ashamed of the gospel of Christ, for it is the power of God to salvation for everyone who believes.

ROMANS 1:16

*S*atan knows God's Word is effective, and that's why he tries to stop it whenever he can. In Luke 8, God's Word is compared to a seed, which Satan does his best to take away or choke out with weeds.

In spite of Satan's schemes, God's Word remains quick and powerful, so sharp it cuts us wide open to reveal our real motives (HEBREWS 4:12). In Jeremiah 23:29 God asks: "Is not My word like a fire? . . . And like a hammer that breaks the rock in pieces?" Who can forget Paul's bold, offensive statement in Romans 1:16: "I am not ashamed of the gospel of Christ, for it is the power of God to salvation for everyone who believes."

Study your Bible so you can wield your sword precisely and effectively. The more you know the Word, the better you can march through Satan's kingdom, cutting right through his core of lies.

From *Unleashing God's Word in Your Life*

Scripture Must Be Our Dearest Study

Be diligent to present yourself approved to God, a worker who does not need to be ashamed, rightly dividing the word of truth.

2 TIMOTHY 2:15

*Your word is a lamp to my feet
And a light to my path.*

PSALM 119:105

Give attention to reading, to exhortation, to doctrine.

1 TIMOTHY 4:13

*Oh, how I love Your law!
It is my meditation all the day.*

PSALM 119:97

All Scripture is given by inspiration of God, and is profitable for doctrine, for reproof, for correction, for instruction in righteousness.

2 TIMOTHY 3:16

As newborn babes, desire the pure milk of the word, that you may grow thereby.

1 PETER 2:2

*Your word I have hidden in my heart,
That I might not sin against You.*

PSALM 119:11

*T*he Bible affirms that people will be held eternally accountable for disobeying the teachings contained therein (PSALM 50:16—17; PROVERBS 13:13; ISAIAH 5:24; LUKE 24:25; 2 TIMOTHY 4:3—4) and that obedience to those words will result in temporal and eternal blessedness (JAMES 1:18; 2 TIMOTHY 3:15—16). Jesus commanded His contemporaries to "search the Scriptures" (JOHN 5:39).

Although there may be several applications of any given passage of Scripture, there is but one true interpretation. The meaning is found as one diligently applies the literal, grammatical-historical method of interpretation under the enlightenment of the Holy Spirit (JOHN 7:17; 16:12—15; 1 CORINTHIANS 2:7—15; 1 JOHN 2:20). Believers are responsible for ascertaining the intent and meaning of Scripture, recognizing that proper application is binding on all generations.

Although many people seem to be intimidated by true Bible study, the Scriptures repeatedly claim to be plain and accessible. In fact, the messages and books of the Bible are addressed in context to people with the expectation that people will obey and understand, and the message of Scripture is so plain that the recipients were commanded to teach them to their children (DEUTERONOMY 6:7).

From *The MacArthur Study Bible* and
Introduction to Biblical Counseling

What is man that You are
mindful of him,
And the son of man that
You visit him?
For You have made him a
little lower than the angels,
And You have crowned him
with glory and honor.

PSALM 8:4–5

THE TRUTH ABOUT PEOPLE

*Once we begin to have a right view
of God and His Word, we can develop a
right perspective of ourselves as humans.
We're fallen, mortal creatures. Talking
dust. But because God has placed a
spark of His eternal spirit in us, we have
inestimable value. He loves us. Us!
Our entire lives should be a response to
God's love* (MARK 12:30).

We Are Created in God's Image

Then God said, "Let Us make man in Our image, according to Our likeness."

GENESIS 1:26

In the day that God created man, He made him in the likeness of God.

GENESIS 5:1

In the image of God He made man.

GENESIS 9:6

With [our tongue] we bless our God and Father, and with it we curse men, who have been made in the similitude of God.

JAMES 3:9

People were created to bear the likeness of our Maker. "Let Us make man in Our image, according to Our likeness" (GENESIS 1:26). This sets us apart from every other creature in the physical universe.

When God created man He immediately said that it was not good for man to be alone. The image of God is personhood, and personhood can function only in the context of relationships. Man's capacity for intimate personal relationships needed fulfillment. Most important, man was designed to have a personal relationship with God.

The truth that humanity was made in the likeness of God is the starting point for a biblical understanding of the nature of man. It explains our spiritual urges. It helps us make sense of the human conscience. It establishes our moral accountability. It reveals the very essence of the meaning and purpose of human life. It is full of practical and doctrinal significance.

From *The Battle for the Beginning*

We Are Mortal

The wages of sin is death.

ROMANS 6:23

Man who is born of woman
Is of few days and full of trouble.
He comes forth like a flower and fades away;
He flees like a shadow and does not continue. . . .
But man dies and is laid away;
Indeed he breathes his last.

JOB 14:1–2, 10

No one has power over the spirit to retain the spirit,
And no one has power in the day of death.
There is no release from that war.

ECCLESIASTES 8:8

Flesh and blood cannot inherit the kingdom of God; nor does
corruption inherit incorruption. . . . For this corruptible must
put on incorruption, and this mortal must put on immortality.
So when this corruptible has put on incorruption, and this
mortal has put on immortality, then shall be brought to pass the
saying that is written: "Death is swallowed up in victory."

1 CORINTHIANS 15:50.

53—54

*T*he germ of death inhabits us all. Because of the curse of sin, we begin to die as soon as we are born. But for the Christian, there is more to this earthly life than death: "If Christ is in you, though the body is dead because of sin, yet the spirit is alive because of righteousness" (ROMANS 8:10 NASB). In other words, the human body is subject to death (and is already dying) because of sin, but the believer's spirit is already alive in Christ. Eternal life is our present possession. Though the body is dying, the spirit is already endowed with incorruptibility.

Paul's point is that the body apart from the Spirit of God has no future. It is subject to death. Therefore we have no duty to the mortal side of our beings (ROMANS 8:12–13). Paul is simply reiterating what he says again and again throughout his New Testament epistles—that those whose lives and hearts are altogether fleshly are not true Christians. They are already spiritually dead, and unless they repent they are headed for eternal death. Meanwhile, their earthly lives are a kind of abject bondage to sin. They are enslaved to their own flesh, constrained to cater to its sensual desires.

But we, in Christ, are not entirely at sin's mercy, as was the case under our former bondage. "Walk by the Spirit, and you will not carry out the desire of the flesh" (GALATIANS 5:16 NASB).

From *The Vanishing Conscience*

Original Sin Makes Us Totally Depraved

Through one man sin entered the world, and death through sin, and thus death spread to all men, because all sinned. . . . For as by one man's disobedience many were made sinners, so also by one Man's obedience many will be made righteous.

ROMANS 5:12, 19

For since by man came death, by Man also came the resurrection of the dead. For as in Adam all die, even so in Christ all shall be made alive.

1 CORINTHIANS 15:21—22

To be carnally minded is death, but to be spiritually minded is life and peace. Because the carnal mind is enmity against God; for it is not subject to the law of God, nor indeed can be. So then, those who are in the flesh cannot please God.

ROMANS 8:6—8

The natural man does not receive the things of the Spirit of God, for they are foolishness to him; nor can he know them, because they are spiritually discerned.

1 CORINTHIANS 2:14

*S*cripture teaches from beginning to end that all humanity is *totally depraved*. Paul says unredeemed people are "dead in … trespasses and sins" (EPHESIANS 2:1 NASB). Apart from salvation, all people walk in worldliness and disobedience (V. 2). We who know and love the Lord once "lived in the lusts of our flesh, indulging the desires of the flesh and of the mind, and were by nature children of wrath, even as the rest" (V. 3 NASB).

In those passages Paul describes the state of unbelievers as estrangement from God. It is that they *hate* God, not that they are intimidated by Him. In fact, Paul says, "There is no fear of God" in the unregenerate person (ROMANS 3:18). Before our salvation, we were actually God's enemies (ROMANS 5:8, 10). We were "alienated and hostile in mind, engaged in evil deeds" (COLOSSIANS 1:21 NASB).

Theologians refer to this doctrine as *total depravity*. It does not mean that unbelieving sinners are always as bad as they could be. It does not mean that the expression of sinful human nature is always lived out to the fullest. It does not mean that unbelievers are incapable of acts of kindness, benevolence, goodwill, or human altruism. It certainly does not mean that non-Christians cannot appreciate goodness, beauty, honesty, decency, or excellence. It *does* mean that none of this has any merit with God.

From *Introduction to Biblical Counseling*

Sin Destroys Us

The wages of sin is death.

ROMANS 6:23

Truly the hearts of the sons of men are full of evil; madness is in their hearts while they live, and after that they go to the dead.

ECCLESIASTES 9:3

We are all like an unclean thing,
And all our righteousnesses are like filthy rags;
We all fade as a leaf,
And our iniquities, like the wind,
Have taken us away.

ISAIAH 64:6

Out of the heart proceed evil thoughts, murders, adulteries, fornications, thefts, false witness, blasphemies. These are the things which defile a man.

MATTHEW 15:19—20

Sin makes true peace impossible for unbelievers: "The wicked are like the tossing sea, for it cannot be quiet, and its waters toss up refuse and mud. 'There is no peace,' says my God, 'for the wicked'" (ISAIAH 57:20–21 NASB).

Sin stains the soul. It degrades a person's nobility. It darkens the mind. It makes us worse than animals, for animals cannot sin. Sin pollutes, defiles, stains. All sin is gross, disgusting, loathsome, revolting in God's sight. Scripture calls it "filthiness" (PROVERBS 30:12; EZEKIEL 24:13; JAMES 1:21). Sin is likened to a putrefying corpse, and sinners are the tombs that contain the stench and foulness (MATTHEW 23:27).

The terrifying consequences of sin include hell, of which Jesus said, "If your right eye makes you stumble, tear it out, and throw it from you; for it is better for you that one of the parts of your body perish, than for your whole body to be thrown into hell" (MATTHEW 5:29).

Scripture describes hell as a dreadful, hideous place where sinners are "tormented with fire and brimstone . . . and the smoke of their torment goes up forever and ever; and they have no rest day and night" (REVELATION 14:10–11 NASB). Those truths become all the more alarming when we realize that they are part of the inspired Word of an infinitely merciful and gracious God.

From *The Vanishing Conscience*

God Has a Plan for Our Salvation

When he prays to God,
he will be accepted.
And God will receive him with joy
and restore him to good standing. . . .
He rescues them from the grave
so they may enjoy the light of life.

JOB 33:26, 30 NLT

For if by the one man's offense judgment came to all men,
resulting in condemnation, even so through one Man's righteous
act the free gift came to all men, resulting in justification of
life.

ROMANS 5:17

Jesus said to him, "I am the way, the truth, and the life. No one
comes to the Father except through Me."

JOHN 14:6

God's intention in the creation of people was that they should glorify God, enjoy His fellowship, live their lives in the will of God, and by this accomplish God's purpose for them in the world. Through Adam's sin of disobedience to the revealed will and Word of God, people lost their innocence, incurred the penalty of spiritual and physical death; became subject to the wrath of God; and became inherently corrupt and utterly incapable of choosing or doing that which is acceptable to God apart from divine grace.

With no recuperative powers to enable them to recover themselves, humans are hopelessly lost. Salvation from sin is thereby wholly of God's grace through the redemptive work of our Lord Jesus Christ.

On the basis of the efficacy of the death of our Lord Jesus Christ, the believing sinner is freed from the punishment, the penalty, the power, and one day the very presence of sin. He or she is declared righteous, given eternal life, and adopted into the family of God.

Every saved person is involved in a daily conflict—the new creation in Christ doing battle against the flesh—but adequate provision is made for victory through the power of the indwelling Holy Spirit. The complete absence of sin is not possible, but the Holy Spirit does provide for victory over sin.

From *MacArthur's Quick Reference Guide to the Bible*

Jesus is God

He who has seen Me has seen the Father . . . The words that I speak to you I do not speak on My own authority; but the Father who dwells in Me does the works. Believe Me that I am in the Father and the Father in Me, or else believe Me for the sake of the works themselves.

JOHN 14:9—11

He is the image of the invisible God, the firstborn over all creation.

COLOSSIANS 1:15

For in Him dwells all the fullness of the Godhead bodily.

COLOSSIANS 2:9

While Jesus was on earth there was much confusion about who He was. Some thought He was a wise man or a great prophet. Others thought He was a madman. Still others couldn't decide or didn't care. But Jesus said, "I and My Father are one" (JOHN 10:30). That means He claimed to be nothing less than God in human flesh.

Many people today don't understand that Jesus claimed to be God. They're content to think of Him as little more than a great moral teacher. But even His enemies understood His claims to deity. That's why they tried to stone Him to death (JOHN 5:18; 10:33) and eventually had Him crucified (JOHN 19:7).

Jesus stated in the clearest possible language that He is God. Christ and His Father are of the same essence (JOHN 14:7). To know Christ is to know the Father, because the different Persons of the Trinity are one in their very essence. Jesus *is* God. To see Him is to see God.

From *www.gty.org* and *Twelve Ordinary Men*

Jesus is Our Substitute

For He made Him who knew no sin to be sin for us, that we might become the righteousness of God in Him.

2 CORINTHIANS 5:21

Surely He has borne our griefs
And carried our sorrows;
Yet we esteemed Him stricken,
Smitten by God, and afflicted.
But He was wounded for our transgressions,
He was bruised for our iniquities;
The chastisement for our peace was upon Him,
And by His stripes we are healed.
All we like sheep have gone astray;
We have turned, every one, to his own way;
And the LORD has laid on Him the iniquity of us all.

ISAIAH 53:4—6

[He] Himself bore our sins in His own body on the tree, that we, having died to sins, might live for righteousness—by whose stripes you were healed.

1 PETER 2:24

God demonstrates His own love toward us, in that while we were still sinners, Christ died for us.

ROMANS 5:8

*T*he substitutionary death of Jesus Christ is an essential truth of the Christian faith. Redemption, justification, reconciliation, removal of sin, and propitiation are all corollaries of Christ's substitutionary work.

The apostle Paul also emphasized this work when he said that God "made Him who knew no sin to be sin for us, that we might become the righteousness of God in Him" (2 CORINTHIANS 5:21), and that "Christ has redeemed us from the curse of the law, having become a curse for us" (GALATIANS 3:13).

Some people claim it's immoral to teach that God would take on human flesh and bear the sins of men and women in their stead. They say it's unfair to transfer the penalty of sin from a guilty person to an innocent person. But that's not what happened. Christ willingly took on our sin and bore its penalty. If He had not willed to take our sin and accept its punishment, as sinners we would have borne the punishment of sin in hell forever. Christ's work on the Cross wasn't unfair—it was God's love in action!

From *Truth for Today*

Jesus Died on the Cross

Jesus of Nazareth, a Man attested by God to you by miracles, wonders, and signs which God did through Him in your midst, as you yourselves also know—Him, being delivered by the determined purpose and foreknowledge of God, you have taken by lawless hands, have crucified, and put to death; . . . Therefore let all the house of Israel know assuredly that God has made this Jesus, whom you crucified, both Lord and Christ.

ACTS 2:22–23, 36

We see Jesus, who was made a little lower than the angels, for the suffering of death crowned with glory and honor, that He, by the grace of God, might taste death for everyone.

HEBREWS 2:9

Do not be afraid; I am the First and the Last. I am He who lives, and was dead, and behold, I am alive forevermore.

REVELATION 1:17–18

Christ died as no other man has ever died. In one sense He was murdered by the hands of wicked men (ACTS 2:23). In another sense it was the Father who sent Him to the Cross and bruised Him there, putting Him to grief—and it pleased the Father to do so (ISAIAH 53:10). Yet in still another sense, no one took Christ's life. He gave it up willingly for those whom He loved (JOHN 10:17–18).

Because of the death He died, suffering the penalty of sin on our behalf, we become partakers with Him in His resurrection as well—that is, if He died in our place and in our stead—then "we believe that we shall also live with Him" (ROMANS 6:8).

It is the Cross that gives meaning to the resurrection life. Only insofar as we are united with Him in the likeness of His death, can we be certain of being raised with Him in the likeness of His resurrection (ROMANS 6:5).

That is why "Jesus Christ and Him crucified" remains the very heart and soul of the gospel message. And in the words of the apostle Paul, every believer's deepest yearning should be this: "That I may know Him and the power of His resurrection, and the fellowship of His sufferings, being conformed to His death, if, by any means, I may attain to the resurrection from the dead" (PHILIPPIANS 3:10–11).

From *The Murder of Jesus*

Jesus Rose from the Dead

This Jesus God has raised up, of which we are all witnesses.

ACTS 2:32

If the Spirit of Him who raised Jesus from the dead dwells in you, He who raised Christ from the dead will also give life to your mortal bodies through His Spirit who dwells in you.

ROMANS 8:11

And with great power the apostles gave witness to the resurrection of the Lord Jesus. And great grace was upon them all.

ACTS 4:33

And if Christ is not risen, your faith is futile; you are still in your sins!

1 CORINTHIANS 15:17

Who is he who condemns? It is Christ who died, and furthermore is also risen, who is even at the right hand of God, who also makes intercession for us.

ROMANS 8:34

He has appointed a day on which He will judge the world in righteousness by the Man whom He has ordained. He has given assurance of this to all by raising Him from the dead.

ACTS 17:31

Christ is risen from the dead, and has become the firstfruits of those who have fallen asleep.

1 CORINTHIANS 15:20

*I*f there was ever any question that Jesus was the Son of God, His resurrection from the dead should end it. He had to be man to reach us, but He had to be God to lift us up. When God raised Christ from the dead, He affirmed that what He said was true.

As clearly as the horizon divides the earth from the sky, so the Resurrection divides Jesus from the rest of humanity. Jesus Christ is God in human flesh. Jesus took on a role requiring voluntary submission, and He did the will of the Father through the power of the Spirit. That is an amazing act of love and humility from One who is fully God and always will be throughout eternity.

It is important to recognize the Spirit's work in the ministry and resurrection of Jesus because it indicates that the entire Trinity was involved in the redemption of mankind. The greatest affirmation that Jesus is who He claimed to be is that the Father raised the Son through the agency of the Holy Spirit.

From *Truth for Today*

Jesus is the Savior

Grow in the grace and knowledge of our Lord and Savior Jesus Christ.

2 PETER 3:18

An entrance will be supplied to you abundantly into the everlasting kingdom of our Lord and Savior Jesus Christ.

2 PETER 1:11

Our Savior Jesus Christ, who has abolished death and brought life and immortality to light through the gospel.

2 TIMOTHY 1:10

Him God has exalted to His right hand to be Prince and Savior, to give repentance to Israel and forgiveness of sins.

ACTS 5:31

We ourselves have heard Him and we know that this is indeed the Christ, the Savior of the world.

JOHN 4:42

*O*ur failure to obey God—to be holy—places us in danger of eternal punishment (2 THESSALONIANS 1:9). The truth is, we cannot obey Him because we have neither the desire nor the ability to do so. We are by nature rebellious toward God (EPHESIANS 2:1–3). The Bible calls our rebellion "sin."

According to Scripture, everyone is guilty of sin: "There is no one who does not sin" (1 KINGS 8:46). "All have sinned and fall short of the glory of God" (ROMANS 3:23). And we are incapable of changing our sinful condition. Jeremiah 13:23 says, "Can the Ethiopian change his skin or the leopard its spots? Then may you also do good who are accustomed to do evil."

Jesus is the only one who can forgive and transform us, thereby delivering us from the power and penalty of sin: "There is salvation in no one else; for there is no other name under heaven that has been given among men, by which we must be saved" (ACTS 4:12 NASB). He alone is "our great God and Savior" (TITUS 2:13 NASB).

From *www.gty.org*

Jesus is the Only Way to Saving Faith

There is born to you this day in the city of David a Savior, who is Christ the Lord.

LUKE 2:11

By grace you have been saved through faith, and that not of yourselves; it is the gift of God, not of works, lest anyone should boast.

EPHESIANS 2:8—9

I am the way, the truth, and the life. No one comes to the Father except through Me.

JOHN 14:6

Jesus said to them again, "Most assuredly, I say to you, I am the door of the sheep. All who ever came before Me are thieves and robbers, but the sheep did not hear them. I am the door. If anyone enters by Me, he will be saved, and will go in and out and find pasture. The thief does not come except to steal, and to kill, and to destroy. I have come that they may have life, and that they may have it more abundantly."

JOHN 10:7—10

*T*he biblical message is clear. Jesus said, "I am the way, the truth, and the life. No one comes to the Father except through Me" (JOHN 14:6). The apostle Peter proclaimed to a hostile audience, "Nor is there salvation in any other, for there is no other name under heaven given among men by which we must be saved" (ACTS 4:12). The apostle John wrote, "He who does not believe the Son shall not see life, but the wrath of God abides on him" (JOHN 3:36).

Again and again, Scripture stresses that Jesus Christ is the only hope of salvation for the world. "For there is one God and one Mediator between God and men, the Man Christ Jesus" (1 TIMOTHY 2:5). Only Christ can atone for sin, and therefore only Christ can provide salvation. "And this is the testimony: that God has given us eternal life, and this life is in His Son. He who has the Son has life; he who does not have the Son of God does not have life" (1 JOHN 5:11—12).

Christianity, as the world's only true religion, is the only one that provides a genuine savior, and that Savior is Jesus. He affirmed that when He declared, "'For the Son of Man has come to seek and to save that which was lost'" (LUKE 19:10).

From *God in the Manger*

Jesus is Lord

God has made this Jesus, whom you crucified, both Lord and Christ.

ACTS 2:36

The word which God sent to the children of Israel, preaching peace through Jesus Christ—He is Lord of all—that word you know.

ACTS 10:36—37

Believe on the Lord Jesus Christ, and you will be saved, you and your household.

ACTS 16:31

Having been justified by faith, we have peace with God through our Lord Jesus Christ.

ROMANS 5:1

Keep yourselves in the love of God, looking for the mercy of our Lord Jesus Christ unto eternal life.

JUDE 21

Grow in the grace and knowledge of our Lord and Savior Jesus Christ. To Him be the glory both now and forever. Amen.

2 PETER 3:18

*R*omans 10:9 says, "If you confess with your mouth the Lord Jesus and believe in your heart that God has raised Him from the dead, you will be saved." Believing that God has raised Him from the dead involves trusting in the historical fact of His resurrection—the pinnacle of Christian faith and the way the Father affirmed the deity and authority of the Son (ROMANS 1:4; ACTS 17:30—31).

It isn't enough to believe certain facts about Christ. Even Satan and his demons believe in the true God (JAMES 2:19), but they don't love and obey Him. Their faith is not genuine. True saving faith always responds in obedience (EPHESIANS 2:10). Confessing Jesus as Lord means humbly submitting to His authority (PHILIPPIANS 2:10—11).

Jesus is the sovereign Lord. When you obey Him you are acknowledging His lordship and submitting to His authority. That doesn't mean your obedience will always be perfect, but that is your goal. There is no area of your life that you withhold from Him.

From *www.gty.org*

Jesus is the Judge

God will judge the secrets of men by Jesus Christ.

ROMANS 2:16

I charge you therefore before God and the Lord Jesus Christ, who will judge the living and the dead at His appearing and His kingdom: Preach the word!

2 TIMOTHY 4:1–2

I can of Myself do nothing. As I hear, I judge; and My judgment is righteous, because I do not seek My own will but the will of the Father who sent Me.

JOHN 5:30

He who believes in Him is not condemned; but He who does not believe is condemned already, because he has not believed in the name of the only begotten Son of God.

JOHN 3:18

All who reject Jesus as their Lord and Savior will one day face Him as their Judge: "God is now declaring to men that all everywhere should repent, because He has fixed a day in which He will judge the world in righteousness through a Man whom He has appointed, having furnished proof to all men by raising Him from the dead" (ACTS 17:30—31 NASB).

God, the ultimate Judge, has justified us in Christ, made us heirs with Him, and has given us His Spirit to ensure that the good work He started in us will be perfected (PHILIPPIANS 1:6). He is able to keep us from stumbling, and to make us "stand in the presence of His glory blameless with great joy" (JUDE 24). Not even Satan himself can condemn us (ROMANS 8:33), so rather than fearing the loss of our inheritance we should continually rejoice in God's great grace and mercy.

As faithful as Jesus is to save those who believe in Him (JOHN 3:16), He is equally faithful to judge those who do not (JOHN 3:18). To act any other way would be inconsistent with His holy, unchangeable nature (HEBREWS 10:23).

From *Our Sufficiency in Christ*
and *The God Who Loves*

We Must Become Righteous

There is therefore now no condemnation to those who are in Christ Jesus, who do not walk according to the flesh, but according to the Spirit. . . . If Christ is in you, the body is dead because of sin, but the Spirit is life because of righteousness.

ROMANS 8:1, 10

Therefore, if anyone is in Christ, he is a new creation; old things have passed away; behold, all things have become new.

2 CORINTHIANS 5:17

As you therefore have received Christ Jesus the Lord, so walk in Him, rooted and built up in Him and established in the faith, as you have been taught, abounding in it with thanksgiving.

COLOSSIANS 2:6—7

Whoever abides in Him does not sin. Whoever sins has neither seen Him nor known Him.

1 JOHN 3:6

"*R*ighteousness" (in Greek, *dikaiosunē*), refers to right behavior toward both God and man. The reference here is not to imputed righteousness received at salvation, but to the practical righteousness to be exhibited in our lives.

Throughout the book of Proverbs, God's redeemed people are called "the righteous." Those whom the Lord loves are those who pursue righteousness (PROVERBS 15:9).

Righteousness as the mark of a true believer is also the lesson of the New Testament. In the Sermon on the Mount, Jesus described true believers as those who hunger and thirst for righteousness (MATTHEW 5:6), and He warned His hearers that "unless your righteousness surpasses that of the scribes and Pharisees, you shall not enter the kingdom of heaven" (MATTHEW 5:20 NASB). First John 3:10 sums it up: "By this the children of God and the children of the devil are obvious: anyone who does not practice righteousness is not of God."

If righteousness is the mark of a true Christian, how much more must it characterize the man of God! He must be like Timothy, whom Paul exhorted "in speech, conduct, love, faith and purity, show yourself an example of those who believe" (1 TIMOTHY 4:12 NASB). The psalmist said it specifically: "He who walks in a blameless way is the one who will minister to me" (PSALM 101:6 NASB).

From *Rediscovering Expository Preaching*

We Can't Become Righteous on Our Own

For He made Him who knew no sin to be sin for us, that we might become the righteousness of God in Him.

2 CORINTHIANS 5:21

I have been crucified with Christ; it is no longer I who live, but Christ lives in me; and the life which I now live in the flesh I live by faith in the Son of God, who loved me and gave Himself for me.

GALATIANS 2:20

Having been justified by faith, we have peace with God through our Lord Jesus Christ, through whom also we have access by faith into this grace in which we stand, and rejoice in hope of the glory of God.

ROMANS 5:1–2 NASB

He shall pray to God, and He will delight in him,
He shall see His face with joy,
For He restores to man His righteousness.

JOB 33:26

And [Abraham] believed in the LORD, and He accounted it to him for righteousness.

GENESIS 15:6

*T*o know Jesus Christ is to have His righteousness, His holiness, and His virtue imputed to us, which makes us right before God.

Throughout his earlier life, the apostle Paul tried to attain salvation through strict adherence to the Law. But when he was confronted by the wondrous reality of Christ, he was ready to trade in all his self-righteous and external morals, good works, and religious rituals for the righteousness granted to him through faith in Christ. Paul was willing to lose the thin and fading robe of his reputation if he could only gain the splendid and incorruptible robe of the righteousness of Christ.

This is the greatest of all benefits because it secures our standing before God. It is God's gift to the sinner, appropriated by faith in the perfect work of Christ, which satisfies God's justice.

From *Truth for Today*

We Must Repent

Jesus began to preach and to say, "Repent, for the kingdom of heaven is at hand."

MATTHEW 4:17

If My people who are called by My name will humble themselves, and pray and seek My face, and turn from their wicked ways, then I will hear from heaven, and will forgive their sin and heal their land.

2 CHRONICLES 7:14

Create in me a clean heart, O God,
And renew a steadfast spirit within me.
Do not cast me away from Your presence,
And do not take Your Holy Spirit from me.
Restore to me the joy of Your salvation,
And uphold me by Your generous Spirit.
Then I will teach transgressors Your ways,
And sinners shall be converted to You.

PSALM 51:10—13

There is joy in the presence of the angels of God over one sinner who repents.

LUKE 15:10

*R*epentance is at the heart of the gospel call. Our Lord demanded that "repentance and remission of sins should be preached in His name to all nations" (LUKE 24:47). If we fail to call people to turn from their sins, we are not communicating the same gospel the apostles proclaimed. It is entirely biblical for the church to make repentance the chief feature of its message to the unsaved world. After all, the gospel calls people to come to the One who can deliver them from *sin*. People who don't feel guilt and want to be delivered from the power and penalty of sin wouldn't even want a deliverer.

To embrace Jesus by saving faith and enter His Kingdom, you must allow Him to expose your sin. That means you repent of your evil thoughts and deeds, come to Him for forgiveness, receive His justification, and begin to live a holy life. But if you hate Jesus for exposing your sin and refuse to repent, you'll die in your sins and go to hell.

From *The Gospel According to the Apostles*
and *God in the Manger*

We Can Be Forgiven

This is My blood of the new covenant, which is shed for many for the remission of sins.

MATTHEW 26:28

In Him we have redemption through His blood, the forgiveness of sins, according to the riches of His grace.

EPHESIANS 1:7

If we confess our sins, He is faithful and just to forgive us our sins and to cleanse us from all unrighteousness.

1 JOHN 1:9

Your sins are forgiven you for His name's sake.

1 JOHN 2:12

*T*he smallest sin is so exceedingly vile that God—despite His infinite mercy, grace, and forgiveness—will not and cannot overlook even one sin without exacting its full penalty, but the cross of Christ provided the solution by enabling the only Perfect Sacrifice to atone for human sin once for all. Our Lord, the sinless One, was the Lamb of God to be offered up as a sacrifice for our sin (JOHN 1:29), and in the same way that our sins were imputed to Him, so His righteousness is reckoned to us who believe: "[God] made Him who knew no sin *to be* sin for us, that we might become the righteousness of God in Him." (2 CORINTHIANS 5:21).

How does a sinner obtain forgiveness and acquire the perfect righteousness of Christ? By being born again (JOHN 3:3). Jesus explained, "Unless one is born of water and the Spirit, he cannot enter the kingdom of God. That which is born of the flesh is flesh, and that which is born of the Spirit is spirit. Do not marvel that I said to you, 'You must be born again.'" (VV. 5–7). Jesus was talking about a spiritual rebirth, a regenerative act of God. This is not something a sinner can accomplish for himself. It is a sovereign work of the Spirit of God, which cannot be controlled by human means. Salvation is wholly God's work.

From *The Vanishing Conscience*

We Can Be Restored

He restores my soul;
He leads me in the paths of righteousness
For His name's sake.

PSALM 23:3

Return, you backsliding children,
And I will heal your backslidings.

JEREMIAH 3:22

We then who are strong ought to bear with the scruples of the weak, and not to please ourselves. . . . Therefore receive one another, just as Christ also received us, to the glory of God.

ROMANS 15:1, 7

If anyone among you wanders from the truth, and someone turns him back, let him know that he who turns a sinner from the error of his way will save a soul from death and cover a multitude of sins.

JAMES 5:19–20

*A*fter he denied Christ, Peter had to face Jesus Christ and have his love questioned. Jesus asked him three times, "Do you love Me?" and Peter was deeply grieved (JOHN 21:17). Of course he loved Christ, and that is why he returned to Him and was restored.

We are all sinners, and choosing sin is denial of Christ. In Romans 15, Paul outlined a three-step process for restoring sinning members of the Body to spiritual health: pick them up, hold them up, and build them up. Before someone who has fallen into sin can get back in the Christian race, that person must first be picked up. Those caught in sin's vicious grasp need help to get back on their feet spiritually through confession of sin and repentance. Those who are spiritually strong also must also help hold up the weaker brethren as they get back on their feet. Those who have just confessed and turned from their sin are extremely vulnerable to further temptation. Satan launches his most savage attacks after a spiritual victory. Those delivered from the grasp of a stubborn sin often need further encouragement, counsel, and, above all, prayer. Finally, after picking up and holding up sinning believers, the spiritually strong must build them up with deeper study of the Word.

From *The Gospel According to the Apostles*
and *Introduction to Biblical Counseling*

We Can Know God's Will for Our Lives

The Lord is not slack concerning His promise, as some count slackness, but is longsuffering toward us, not willing that any should perish but that all should come to repentance.

2 PETER 3:9

See then that you walk circumspectly, not as fools but as wise, redeeming the time, because the days are evil. Therefore do not be unwise, but understand what the will of the Lord is. And do not be drunk with wine, in which is dissipation; but be filled with the Spirit, speaking to one another in psalms and hymns and spiritual songs, singing and making melody in your heart to the Lord, giving thanks always for all things to God the Father in the name of our Lord Jesus Christ, submitting to one another in the fear of God.

EPHESIANS 5:15—21

This is the will of God, your sanctification: that you should abstain from sexual immorality; that each of you should know how to possess his own vessel in sanctification and honor.

1 THESSALONIANS 4:3-4

Submit yourselves to every ordinance of man for the Lord's sake, whether to the king as supreme, or to governors, as to those who are sent by him for the punishment of evildoers and for the praise of those who do good. For this is the will of God, that by doing good you may put to silence the ignorance of foolish men.

1 PETER 2:13—15

$\mathcal{T}$here is a lot of concern and confusion about God's will, but it need not remain a mystery. There are many good formulas and systems for learning God's will. But the best system is simply reading the Bible and finding out what it teaches about God's will:

He wants us to be saved (2 PETER. 3:9).
He wants us to be Spirit-filled (EPHESIANS 5:15—18).
He wants us to be sanctified (1 THESSALONIANS 4:3—4).
He wants us to be submissive (1 PETER 2:13—15).
He wants us to be willing to suffer for His sake (1 PETER 4:12—19).

About now you might be saying, "All these biblical principles are fine, but they're general. What about taking a new job, picking a mate, buying a new car or house, and the million other decisions that involve my Christian walk and testimony?"

Well, I've got one other principle for doing God's will, and it may sound too good to be true. If you are saved, Spirit-filled, sanctified, submissive, and willing to suffer, do whatever you want. If you are obeying God's Word in the five areas discussed in this chapter, God is *already* controlling your wants and desires. He is at work "in you both to will and to do for *His* good pleasure" (PHILIPPIANS 2:13). If you "delight . . . in the LORD," He will give you "the desires of your heart" (PSALM 37:4) because they will be His desires for you.

From *Unleashing God's Will for Your Life*

We Should Be Godly

As He who called you is holy, you also be holy in all your conduct, because it is written, "Be holy, for I am holy."

1 PETER 1:15—16

Let us cleanse ourselves from all filthiness of the flesh and spirit, perfecting holiness in the fear of God.

2 CORINTHIANS 7:1

Godliness is profitable for all things, having promise of the life that now is and of that which is to come.

1 TIMOTHY 4:8

Godliness with contentment is great gain. . . . Pursue righteousness, godliness, faith, love, patience, gentleness.

1 TIMOTHY 6:6, 11

"*G*odliness" (in Greek, *eusebeia*) is closely connected with righteousness. Righteousness may speak of outward conduct, godliness of the inward attitude. Godliness is the spirit of holiness, reverence, and piety that directs righteous behavior. Right behavior flows from a right attitude; correct conduct flows from proper motive.

The basic meaning of *eusebeia* is reverence for God. The man characterized by *eusebeia* has a worshiping heart. He knows what it means to "live in the fear of the LORD always" (PROVERBS 23:17). He not only does right, but also thinks right; he not only behaves properly, but also is properly motivated. He is a man who serves God with reverence and awe (HEBREWS 12:28).

Righteousness and godliness are together the two indispensable qualities of a man of God, and yet they are his lifelong pursuit. They are central to his usefulness; they are at the core of his power. He possesses them and yet pursues them.

A man of God must constantly guard his heart, his motives, his desires, and his conduct, knowing that nothing good dwells in his flesh (ROMANS 7:18). He must "cleanse [himself] from all defilement of flesh and spirit, perfecting holiness in the fear of God" (2 CORINTHIANS 7:1). He must be godly.

From *Rediscovering Expository Preaching*

We Should Abide in Christ

If we love one another, God abides in us, and His love has been perfected in us. By this we know that we abide in Him, and He in us, because He has given us of His Spirit. And we have seen and testify that the Father has sent the Son as Savior of the world. Whoever confesses that Jesus is the Son of God, God abides in him, and he in God. And we have known and believed the love that God has for us. God is love, and he who abides in love abides in God, and God in him.

1 JOHN 4:12—16

Whoever abides in Him does not sin. Whoever sins has neither seen Him nor known Him.

1 JOHN 3:6

Abide in Me, and I in you. As the branch cannot bear fruit of itself, unless it abides in the vine, so neither can you, unless you abide in Me. . . . If you abide in Me, and My words abide in you, you will ask what you desire, and it shall be done for you. By this My Father is glorified, that you bear much fruit; so you will be My disciples.

JOHN 15:4, 7—8

$\mathcal{T}$he word *abide* basically means "to remain." Every Christian remains inseparably linked to Christ in all areas of life. We depend on Him for grace and power to obey. We look obediently to His Word for instruction on how to live. We offer Him our deepest adoration and praise and we submit ourselves to His authority over our lives. In short, Christians gratefully know Jesus Christ is the source and sustainer of their lives.

Abiding in Christ evidences genuine salvation. John alluded to that when he referred to defected professors who "went out from us, but they were not really of us; for if they had been of us, they would have remained with us; but they went out, so that it would be shown that they all are not of us" (1 JOHN 2:19 NASB).

People with genuine faith will remain—they won't defect; they won't deny Christ or abandon His truth. Jesus reiterated the importance of abiding as a sign of real faith when He said, "If you abide in My word, you are My disciples indeed" (JOHN 8:31).

From *www.gty.org*

We Should Live in the Spirit

There is therefore now no condemnation to those who are in Christ Jesus, who do not walk according to the flesh, but according to the Spirit. For the law of the Spirit of life in Christ Jesus has made me free from the law of sin and death. . . . You are not in the flesh but in the Spirit, if indeed the Spirit of God dwells in you. . . . The Spirit Himself bears witness with our spirit that we are children of God.

ROMANS 8:1–2, 9, 16

By this we know that we abide in Him and He in us, because He has given us of His Spirit.

1 JOHN 4:13

Walk in the Spirit, and you shall not fulfill the lust of the flesh.

GALATIANS 5:16

You also are being built together for a dwelling place of God in the Spirit.

EPHESIANS 2:22

*I*n Romans 8 alone there are at least twenty references to the Holy Spirit. This chapter portrays the Holy Spirit as the divine agent who frees us from sin and death (VV. 2—3), enables us to live righteously (VV. 4—13), assures and comforts us in our affliction (VV. 14—19), preserves and sustains us in Christ (VV. 20—28), and guarantees our final victory in eternal glory (VV. 29—39). The Greek word translated "dwells" (V. 9) is *oikeō*, which means "to inhabit." Paul is saying that the very Spirit of God indwells every person who trusts in Jesus Christ.

All true Christians are "in the Spirit." The Holy Spirit changes our basic disposition when we are born again. He brings us into accord with Himself. He actually indwells us (VV. 9, 11). We become partakers of the divine nature (2 PETER 1:4). Our orientation to God changes. In the flesh we could not please God (ROMANS 8:8) but now the righteous requirement of the law is fulfilled in us (V. 4). Central to all of this is the reality that our whole mindset is new. Whereas the mind set on the flesh meant death, the mind set on the things of the Spirit results in life and peace (V. 6).

From *The Vanishing Conscience*

We Should Obey God

Seek first the kingdom of God and His righteousness, and all these things shall be added to you.

MATTHEW 6:33

If anyone loves Me, he will keep My word; and My Father will love him, and We will come to him and make Our home with him.

JOHN 14:23

By this we know that we know Him, if we keep His commandments. He who says, "I know Him," and does not keep His commandments, is a liar, and the truth is not in him. But whoever keeps His word, truly the love of God is perfected in him. By this we know that we are in Him.

1 JOHN 2:3—5

*H*ere's how you can be sure your faith is real: you keep God's commandments. This is a test of obedience. The Greek word translated *keep* in 1 John 2:3–5 conveys the idea of a watchful, observant obedience. It is not an obedience that is only the result of external pressure. It is the eager obedience of one who "keeps" the divine commandments as if they were something precious to guard. In other words, this speaks of an obedience motivated by love. Those who claim to know God yet despise His commandments are liars (v. 4). "They profess to know God, but in works they deny Him, being abominable, disobedient, and disqualified for every good work" (TITUS 1:16).

Wholehearted commitment to Christ does not mean that we never disobey or that we live perfect lives. The vestiges of our sinful flesh make it inevitable that we will often do what we do not want to do (ROMANS 7:15). But commitment to Christ *does* mean that obedience rather than disobedience will be our distinguishing trait. God will deal with the sin in our lives and we will respond to His loving chastisement by becoming more holy (HEBREWS 12:5—11).

From *The Gospel According to the Apostles*

We Should Yield to Christ's Authority

Jesus came and spoke to them, saying, "All authority has been given to Me in heaven and on earth. Go therefore and make disciples of all the nations, baptizing them in the name of the Father and of the Son and of the Holy Spirit, teaching them to observe all things that I have commanded you; and lo, I am with you always, even to the end of the age." Amen.

MATTHEW 28:18—20

Jesus Christ, who has gone into heaven and is at the right hand of God, angels and authorities and powers having been made subject to Him.

1 PETER 3:21—22

When the righteous are in authority, the people rejoice;
But when a wicked man rules, the people groan.

PROVERBS 29:2

*T*he gospel call to faith presupposes that sinners must repent of their sin and yield to Christ's authority. Surrender to Jesus' lordship is not an addendum to the biblical terms of salvation; rather, the summons to submission is at the heart of the gospel invitation throughout Scripture.

Salvation is by grace through faith in the Lord Jesus Christ alone—plus and minus nothing (EPHESIANS 2:8–9). No matter how many good things we do, we cannot earn salvation or favor with God (ROMANS 8:8). However, real faith inevitably produces a changed life (2 CORINTHIANS 5:17). Jesus is Lord of all, and the faith He demands involves unconditional surrender (ROMANS 6:17–18; 10:9–10). Those who truly believe will love Christ (1 PETER 1:8–9; ROMANS 8:28–30; 1 CORINTHIANS 16:22). They will therefore long to obey Him, to yield to His authority (JOHN 14:15, 23).

Jesus as Lord is far more than just an authority figure; He's also our highest treasure and most precious companion. We obey Him out of sheer delight. So the gospel demands surrender, not only for authority's sake, but also because surrender is the believer's highest joy. Such surrender is not an extraneous adjunct to faith; it is the very essence of believing.

From *The Gospel According to the Apostles*

We Will Never Be Perfect

It is God who arms me with strength,
And makes my way perfect.

PSALM 18:32

For there is not a just man on earth who does good
And does not sin.

ECCLESIASTES 7:20

Not that I have already attained, or am already perfected; but
I press on, that I may lay hold of that for which Christ Jesus
has also laid hold of me. Brethren, I do not count myself to
have apprehended; but one thing I do, forgetting those things
which are behind and reaching forward to those things which
are ahead, I press toward the goal for the prize of the upward
call of God in Christ Jesus. Therefore let us, as many as are
mature, have this mind; and if in anything you think otherwise,
God will reveal even this to you.

PHILIPPIANS 3:12–15

For we all stumble in many things.

JAMES 3:2

God's standard of holiness is absolute perfection, but He has graciously made provision for our inevitable failures. If we do something wrong, He doesn't say we are no longer Christians. The harsh reality is that every Christian fails to follow Christ perfectly, because every Christian has a sinful nature. But we are blessed to live in gracious obedience, which is a loving and sincere spirit of submission motivated by God's love for us. Although often defective, this obedience is nevertheless accepted by God, for its blemishes are blotted out by the blood of Jesus Christ.

Although we can't obey God perfectly, we can and do try to pattern our lives after the one Person in history who could obey with perfection—Jesus Christ. He shows us by example what to do if only we will follow Him.

From *Welcome to the Family*

We Should Let God Perfect Us

Love your enemies, bless those who curse you, do good to those who hate you, and pray for those who spitefully use you and persecute you. . . . Therefore you shall be perfect, just as your Father in heaven is perfect.

MATTHEW 5:44, 48

Not that I have already attained, or am already perfected; but I press on, that I may lay hold of that for which Christ Jesus has also laid hold of me.

PHILIPPIANS 3:12

He said to me, "My grace is sufficient for you, for My strength is made perfect in weakness." Therefore most gladly I will rather boast in my infirmities, that the power of Christ may rest upon me.

2 CORINTHIANS 12:9

By one offering He has perfected forever those who are being sanctified.

HEBREWS 10:14

Scripture recognizes that we are not perfect. We all fall short of perfection—way short. Paul teaches us that our own imperfection should only spur us on toward the goal of complete Christlikeness. We must continue to press on toward the goal: "Be perfect, as your heavenly Father is perfect" (MATTHEW 5:48 NASB).

Peter writes, "After you have suffered for a little while, the God of all grace, who called you to His eternal glory in Christ, will Himself perfect, confirm, strengthen and establish you" (1 PETER 5:10 NASB).

Can you grasp the magnitude of that promise? *God Himself* perfects, confirms, strengthens, and establishes His children. Though His purposes for the future involve some pain in the present, He will nevertheless give us grace to endure and persevere. Even while we are being personally attacked by the enemy, we are being personally perfected by God. He Himself is doing it.

He will accomplish His purposes in us, bringing us to wholeness, setting us on solid ground, making us strong, and establishing us on a firm foundation.

From *The Vanishing Conscience*
and *The Gospel According to the Apostles*

We Should Love God

You shall love the LORD your God with all your heart, with all your soul, and with all your strength.

DEUTERONOMY 6:5

Jesus said to him, "'You shall love the LORD your God with all your heart, with all your soul, and with all your mind.' This is the first and great commandment."

MATTHEW 22:37–38

If anyone loves Me, he will keep My word; and My Father will love him, and We will come to him and make Our home with him.

JOHN 14:23

Love suffers long and is kind; love does not envy; love does not parade itself, is not puffed up; does not behave rudely, does not seek its own, is not provoked, thinks no evil; does not rejoice in iniquity, but rejoices in the truth; bears all things, believes all things, hopes all things, endures all things. Love never fails.

1 CORINTHIANS 13:4–8

*T*he heart and soul of the Christian life is our love for Christ. Our salvation begins with Him, our sanctification progresses with Him, and our glorification ends with Him. He is the reason for our being, and thus He is more precious to us than anyone or anything. Jesus enabled us to receive His love because He died for our sin of hating God. Now He enables us to love God, because it is through Him that "the love of God has been poured out in our hearts by the Holy Spirit" (ROMANS 5:5). First John 4:19 confirms this wonderful truth: "We love Him because He first loved us."

Love and trust are inextricably linked in the cycle of Christian growth: God grants you faith, and by faith you grasp the biblical teachings about Jesus Christ. As your knowledge of Him increases, your love and trust grow deeper and stronger. Increasingly you desire to glorify Him by serving Him wholeheartedly, talking and reading about Him, communing with Him, thus getting to know Him better and becoming increasingly like Him.

From *Welcome to the Family*

We Should Be People of Faith

By grace you have been saved through faith, and that not of yourselves; it is the gift of God, not of works, lest anyone should boast.

EPHESIANS 2:8—9

For in it the righteousness of God is revealed from faith to faith; as it is written, "The just shall live by faith."

ROMANS 1:17

Faith is the substance of things hoped for, the evidence of things not seen. . . . Without faith it is impossible to please Him, for he who comes to God must believe that He is, and that He is a rewarder of those who diligently seek Him.

HEBREWS 11:1, 6

*A*s a divine gift, faith is neither transient nor impotent. It has an abiding quality that guarantees that it will endure to the end. The familiar words of Habakkuk 2:4, "The just shall live by his faith" speak not of a momentary act of believing, but of a living, enduring trust in God.

The faith God gives can never evaporate. And the work of salvation cannot ultimately be thwarted. In Philippians 1:6 Paul wrote, "I am confident of this very thing, that He who began a good work in you will perfect it until the day of Christ Jesus."

The faith God graciously supplies produces both the volition and the ability to comply with His will: "it is God who works in you both to will and to do for His good pleasure" (PHILIPPIANS 2:13). Thus faith is inseparable from obedience.

Obedience is the inevitable manifestation of true faith. Paul recognized this when he wrote to Titus about "those who are defiled and unbelieving profess to know God but by their deeds they deny Him" (TITUS 1:15–16 NASB). True faith is manifest only in obedience.

And so the faithful (believing) are also faithful (obedient). "Fidelity, constancy, firmness, confidence, reliance, trust, [and] belief" are all indivisibly wrapped up in the idea of believing. Righteous living is an inevitable byproduct of real faith.

From *Introduction to Biblical Counseling*

We Should Be People of Hope

This hope we have as an anchor of the soul, both sure and steadfast, and which enters the Presence behind the veil.

HEBREWS 6:19

Blessed be the God and Father of our Lord Jesus Christ, who according to His abundant mercy has begotten us again to a living hope through the resurrection of Jesus Christ from the dead, to an inheritance incorruptible and undefiled and that does not fade away, reserved in heaven for you, who are kept by the power of God through faith for salvation ready to be revealed in the last time.

1 PETER 1:3—5

I consider that the sufferings of this present time are not worthy to be compared with the glory which shall be revealed in us. . . . We ourselves groan within ourselves, eagerly waiting for the adoption, the redemption of our body. For we were saved in this hope, but hope that is seen is not hope; for why does one still hope for what he sees? But if we hope for what we do not see, we eagerly wait for it with perseverance.

ROMANS 8:18, 23—25

Blessed is the man who trusts in the LORD,
And whose hope is the LORD.

JEREMIAH 17:7

*E*veryone who trusts in Jesus Christ for salvation from sin has reason to hope. We have a heavenly Father who will never desert us, never deceive us, and always love us. Biblical hope is a fact that God has promised and will fulfill. This hope causes us to look to the future with joy and motivates us to pursue Christlikeness here on earth with maximum effort. Hope is central to a life of faith. Our hope is based on the resurrection of Christ (1 CORINTHIANS 15:17). Our hope is glory (ROMANS 8:18–25). Here are eleven features of true hope that should produce joy in every Christian heart:

1. Our hope comes from God (PSALM 43:5).
2. Our hope is a gift of grace (2 THESSALONIANS 2:16–17).
3. Our hope is defined by Scripture (ROMANS 15:4).
4. Our hope is reasonable (1 PETER 3:15).
5. Our hope is secured by Christ's resurrection (1 PETER 1:3).
6. Our hope is confirmed by the Spirit (ROMANS 15:13).
7. Our hope is a defense against Satan (JOHN 6:37–39).
8. Our hope is strengthened, not weakened, through trials (1 THESSALONIANS 5:8–11).
9. Our hope produces joy (PSALM 146:5).
10. Our hope removes the fear of death (1 CORINTHIANS 15:55–57).
11. Our hope is ultimately fulfilled in Christ's return (1 THESSALONIANS 4:16–17).

From *Welcome to the Family*

We Should Be People of Love

You shall love your neighbor as yourself: I am the LORD.

LEVITICUS 19:18

Behold, how good and how pleasant it is
For brethren to dwell together in unity!

PSALM 133:1

New commandment I give to you, that you love one another; as I have loved you, that you also love one another. By this all will know that you are My disciples, if you have love for one another.

JOHN 13:34—35

Let love be without hypocrisy. Abhor what is evil. Cling to what is good. Be kindly affectionate to one another with brotherly love, in honor giving preference to one another.

ROMANS 12:9—10

God is the source of all true love. Love is therefore the best evidence that a person truly knows God: "Beloved, let us love one another, for love is of God; and everyone who loves is born of God and knows God. He who does not love does not know God, for God is love" (1 JOHN 4:7–8). In other words, love is the proof of a regenerate heart. Only true Christians are capable of genuine love.

Clearly, the kind of love the apostle is speaking of is a higher, purer form of love than we commonly know from human experience. The love of which he speaks does not flow naturally from the human heart. It is not a carnal love, a romantic love, or even a familial love. It is a supernatural love that is peculiar to those who know God. It is *godly* love.

This kind of love cannot be conjured up by the human will. It is wrought in the hearts of believers by God Himself. "We love, because He first loved us" (1 JOHN 4:19). Love for God and love for fellow believers is an inevitable result of the new birth, by which we become "partakers of the divine nature" (2 PETER 1:4).

Godly love, therefore, is one of the most important tests of the reality of one's faith.

From *The God Who Loves*

We Should Be People of Joy

But the fruit of the Spirit is love, joy, peace, longsuffering, kindness, goodness, faithfulness.

GALATIANS 5:22

These things I have spoken to you, that My joy may remain in you, and that your joy may be full.

JOHN 15:11

And these things we write to you that your joy may be full.

1 JOHN 1:4

Rejoice in the Lord always. Again I will say, rejoice!

PHILIPPIANS 4:4

Yet I will rejoice in the LORD, I will joy in the God of my salvation.

HABAKKUK 3:18

Therefore with joy you will draw water from the wells of salvation.

ISAIAH 12:3

Christians have many reasons for rejoicing. The primary one is based on who God is—He is sovereign. That is the single greatest truth about God. Nothing is outside His control, and He controls everything to work out ultimately for our good (ROMANS 8:28). He has an infinite understanding of every aspect of our lives (PSALM 139:2–4). And He exercises His understanding in perfect wisdom. Knowing God like that should give us inexpressible and glorious joy.

We should also rejoice because God saved us, adopted us, and promised to give us an inheritance in Jesus Christ (EPHESIANS 1:1–11). When Christ returns, we will enjoy His presence and the heavenly place He has prepared for us (JOHN 14:2–3). Until then, we have joy in knowing God has promised to supply all our needs (PHILIPPIANS 4:19).

We can also have joy in knowing we can pray to God at any time (HEBREWS 4:15–16). Furthermore, we have the privilege of serving the One we supremely love. That includes sharing the good news with the lost and encouraging fellow Christians to grow in their love and joy in serving Him.

From *Truth for Today*

165

We Should Choose Our Loyalties Carefully

If you were of the world, the world would love its own. Yet because you are not of the world, but I chose you out of the world, therefore the world hates you.

JOHN 15:19

You were once darkness, but now you are light in the Lord. . . . Have no fellowship with the unfruitful works of darkness, but rather expose them.

EPHESIANS 5:8, 11

Do not be unequally yoked together with unbelievers. For what fellowship has righteousness with lawlessness? And what communion has light with darkness? And what accord has Christ with Belial? Or what part has a believer with an unbeliever?

2 CORINTHIANS 6:14—15

Do you not know that friendship with the world is enmity with God? Whoever therefore wants to be a friend of the world makes himself an enemy of God.

JAMES 4:4

Do not love the world or the things in the world. If anyone loves the world, the love of the Father is not in him. For all that is in the world—the lust of the flesh, the lust of the eyes, and the pride of life—is not of the Father but is of the world. And the world is passing away, and the lust of it; but he who does the will of God abides forever.

1 JOHN 2:15—17

*L*oving other Christians is proof of the change God has wrought in your heart. But perhaps the severest trial you will face as a new believer is that people who were once your friends, maybe even members of your earthly family, may now hate you the way the world hated Christ (JOHN 15:17–25). The disciples' love for one another was so important because the world hates them so much.

Following Christ isn't likely to lead many Westerners to martyrdom or exile, but the same hostility toward believers is true in today's world. The culture does not accept Christians because it does not accept the gospel of our Lord. And you cannot evade that hostility without compromising your Christianity. Our lives are to be a rebuke to the sinful world (EPHESIANS 5:11). If you are not experiencing much rejection from the world, your life may not be a rebuke to the world.

The unavoidable fact is that people who don't know Jesus Christ are part of a system that is anti-God, anti-Christ, and satanic. Followers of false religions may have a superficial tolerance of the things of God, but they are tools of Satan in his war against truth. Being persecuted for Jesus is a unique privilege (ACTS 5:41; PHILIPPIANS 3:10) granted to those who truly choose friendship with Christ over friendship with the world and its evil system.

From *Welcome to the Family*

We Should Be Involved in a Church

Let us consider one another in order to stir up love and good works, not forsaking the assembling of ourselves together, as is the manner of some, but exhorting one another, and so much the more as you see the Day approaching.

HEBREWS 10:24—25

If we say that we have fellowship with Him, and walk in darkness, we lie and do not practice the truth. But if we walk in the light as He is in the light, we have fellowship with one another, and the blood of Jesus Christ His Son cleanses us from all sin.

1 JOHN 1:6—7

Now, therefore, you are no longer strangers and foreigners, but fellow citizens with the saints and members of the household of God, having been built on the foundation of the apostles and prophets, Jesus Christ Himself being the chief cornerstone, in whom the whole building, being fitted together, grows into a holy temple in the Lord, in whom you also are being built together for a dwelling place of God in the Spirit.

EPHESIANS 2:19—22

*T*he church is not a building—it is a group of worshiping, redeemed, and sanctified people. We need to understand a few basic truths about the church:

1. The church is the only institution that our Lord promised to build and to bless (MATTHEW 16:18).

2. The church is the gathering place of true worshipers (PHILIPPIANS 3:3).

3. The church is the most precious assembly on earth because Christ purchased it with His own blood (ACTS 20:28; 1 CORINTHIANS 6:19; REVELATION 1:5).

4. The church is the earthly expression of the heavenly reality (MATTHEW 6:10; 18:18).

5. The church will ultimately triumph both universally and locally (MATTHEW 16:18; PHILIPPIANS 1:6).

6. The church is the realm of spiritual fellowship (HEBREWS 10:22–25; 1 JOHN 1:3; 6–7).

7. The church is the proclaimer and protector of divine truth (1 TIMOTHY 3:15; TITUS 2:1, 15).

8. The church is the chief place for spiritual edification and growth (ACTS 20:32; EPHESIANS 4:11–16; 2 PETER 3:18).

9. The church is the launching pad for world evangelization (MARK 16:15; TITUS 2:11).

10. The church is the environment where strong spiritual leadership develops and matures (2 TIMOTHY 2:2).

From *Rediscovering Pastoral Ministry*

We Should be Accountable Within a Church

We, being many, are one body in Christ, and individually members of one another.

ROMANS 12:5

If a man is overtaken in any trespass, you who are spiritual restore such a one in a spirit of gentleness, considering yourself lest you also be tempted. Bear one another's burdens, and so fulfill the law of Christ.

GALATIANS 6:1—2

Warn those who are unruly, comfort the fainthearted, uphold the weak, be patient with all. See that no one renders evil for evil to anyone, but always pursue what is good both for yourselves and for all.

1 THESSALONIANS
5:14—15

We command you, brethren, in the name of our Lord Jesus Christ, that you withdraw from every brother who walks disorderly. . . . Note that person and do not keep company with him, that he may be ashamed. Yet do not count him as an enemy, but admonish him as a brother.

2 THESSALONIANS 3:6.
14—15

We all struggle with the same temptations (1 Corinthians 10:13). That is why Paul told the Galatians, "Bear one another's burdens, and so fulfill the law of Christ" (Galatians 6:2). We need each other. Can we keep each other from sinning? Not always. But we can encourage one another (Hebrews 3:13; 1 Thessalonians 5:11). We can stimulate one another to love and good works (Hebrews 10:24–25). And "if a man is overtaken in any trespass, you who *are* spiritual restore such a one in a spirit of gentleness, considering yourself lest you also be tempted" (Galatians 6:1).

This is a very important reason the church was instituted. We are to hold one another accountable, lovingly pursue those who sin (Matthew 18:15–17), love one another, and serve one another. All of this works corporately to help us as individuals mortify our sin and live godly lives. The only true remedy for sin involves humble repentance, confession (the recognition that you deserve the chastening of God because you alone are responsible for your sin)—then restitution, and growth through the spiritual disciplines of prayer, Bible study, communion with God, fellowship with other believers, and dependence on Christ.

From *The Vanishing Conscience*

We Should Confess Our Sin

If we confess our sins, He is faithful and just to forgive us our sins and to cleanse us from all unrighteousness. If we say that we have not sinned, we make Him a liar, and His word is not in us.

1 JOHN 1:9–10

I prayed to the LORD my God, and made confession, and said, "O Lord, great and awesome God, who keeps His covenant and mercy with those who love Him, and with those who keep His commandments, we have sinned and committed iniquity, we have done wickedly and rebelled, even by departing from Your precepts and Your judgments."

DANIEL 9:4–5

On this one will I look:
On him who is poor and of a contrite spirit,
And who trembles at My word.

ISAIAH 66:2

For I will declare my iniquity;
I will be in anguish over my sin.

PSALM 38:18

Confess your trespasses to one another, and pray for one another, that you may be healed. The effective, fervent prayer of a righteous man avails much.

JAMES 5:16

*A*lthough many support groups encourage members to confess their weaknesses, the church is probably the only organization where people meet together regularly to confess their problems specifically with sin itself. All Christians who take honest spiritual inventories are cognizant of personal sin. We know God hates sin and thus we are unnerved over our own iniquities. So Christians continually confess their sin.

The forgiveness we seek in our daily walk is not pardon from an angry Judge, but mercy from a grieved Father. When we are justified in Christ, God has forgiven all our sins already and clothed us in the perfect righteousness of Christ. We already have the judicial forgiveness of justification that makes us right with God as our judge, but the daily forgiveness Jesus taught us to pray for is a familial forgiveness. It is the remedy for God's fatherly displeasure when His children sin (HEBREWS 12:5–11).

As long as we live in a sinful world, with our own sinful tendencies, Christians still need daily cleansing from the defiling influence of our sin. When David sinned with Bathsheba, he confessed his sin to God and then pleaded, "Restore to me the joy of Your salvation" (PSALM 51:12). Notice that David did not ask for his salvation to be restored, but rather the joy of it.

From *Lord, Teach Me to Pray*

We Should Mortify Our Sin

For if you live according to the flesh you will die; but if by the Spirit you put to death the deeds of the body, you will live.

ROMANS 8:13

But put on the Lord Jesus Christ, and make no provision for the flesh, to fulfill its lusts.

ROMANS 13:14

But I discipline my body and bring it into subjection, lest, when I have preached to others, I myself should become disqualified.

1 CORINTHIANS 9:27

Therefore put to death your members which are on the earth: fornication, uncleanness, passion, evil desire, and covetousness, which is idolatry.

COLOSSIANS 3:5

If your hand causes you to sin, cut it off. It is better for you to enter into life maimed, rather than having two hands, to go to hell, into the fire that shall never be quenched.

MARK 9:43

*E*very honest Christian will testify that the tendency to sin is not erased by becoming a believer. We still derive pleasure from sin. We still struggle with sinful habits. Our thoughts are not what they ought to be. Our time is often wasted on frivolous pursuits. Our hearts grow cold to the things of God.

Scripture urges us to put to death—or mortify—our sin and its influence throughout our lifetime. This involves cultivating new habits of godliness while eliminating sinful habits from our behavior. It is a constant warfare that takes place within the believer. We must see sin as a sworn enemy, and commit ourselves to slaying it wherever and whenever it rears its head. The instrument of mortification is the Holy Spirit, and His power is the energy that works in us to carry out the process. Some of the keys to mortification include:

- Abstain from fleshly lusts (1 PETER 2:11; 1 CORINTHIANS 6:18).
- Make no provision for the flesh (ROMANS 13:14).
- Fix your heart on Christ (1 JOHN 3:2-3; 2 CORINTHIANS 3:18).
- Meditate on God's Word (PSALM 119:11; JOSHUA 1:8; COLOSSIANS 3:16).
- Pray without ceasing (LUKE 11:4; 22:40; MATTHEW 26:41).
- Watch and pray (PSALM 19:2-14; 1 JOHN 1:9; HEBREWS 4:6).
- Exercise self-control (GALATIANS 5:23; 1 CORINTHIANS 9:25-27).
- Be filled with the Spirit (EPHESIANS 5:18; ROMANS 8:13).

From *The Vanishing Conscience*

Prayer is Essential for Believers

Be anxious for nothing, but in everything by prayer and supplication, with thanksgiving, let your requests be made known to God; and the peace of God, which surpasses all understanding, will guard your hearts and minds through Christ Jesus.

PHILIPPIANS 4:6—7

In my distress I called upon the LORD,
And cried out to my God;
He heard my voice from His temple,
And my cry came before Him, even to His ears.

PSALM 18:6

Ask, and it will be given to you; seek, and you will find; knock, and it will be opened to you. For everyone who asks receives, and he who seeks finds, and to him who knocks it will be opened.

MATTHEW 7:7—8

Whatever we ask we receive from Him, because we keep His commandments and do those things that are pleasing in His sight. And this is His commandment: that we should believe on the name of His Son Jesus Christ and love one another, as He gave us commandment.

1 JOHN 3:22—23

*P*rayer moves the riches of God's supernatural grace from heaven to earth—from His throne to our need. He will respond to our cries and do what is best for us in each experience of life, while still fulfilling His perfect eternal purpose for us.

Prayer is an intimate privilege through which we have access to unlimited, divine resources from a loving heavenly Father. We are blessed with a boundless treasury of all spiritual blessings in Christ Jesus—some received already; others waiting to be delivered. The access to the riches of God's grace is only by means of prayer: "You do not have because you do not ask" (JAMES 4:2).

Prayer is also a passion. Most of what Scripture teaches about prayer is based on the assumption that a fervent desire for prayer will arise from every believer's heart. The deepest longings of a Spirit-filled heart flow out in prayer. If we examine what we pray for and find we are praying only for our own needs, problems, questions, and struggles—or if we pray infrequently, briefly, and in a shallow manner—we need to do a spiritual inventory to see whether our hearts have grown cold or selfish. When our desires and requests are aligned with and subjugated to the will of God, we know He will hear and grant what we seek of Him. Let the truth of Scripture shape your thinking and feed your appetites, and then you will know how to pray according to the will of God.

From *Lord, Teach Me to Pray*

God Longs to Answer Our Prayers

It shall come to pass
That before they call, I will answer;
And while they are still speaking, I will hear.

ISAIAH 65:24

The eyes of the LORD are on the righteous,
And His ears are open to their cry.

PSALM 34:15

If we ask anything according to His will, He hears us.

1 JOHN 5:14

If you abide in Me, and My words abide in you, you will ask
what you desire, and it shall be done for you.

JOHN 15:7

*F*or God to answer prayer, it has to be offered as the Bible instructs. You can't just pray for a new car or a million dollars and expect God to come through like some cosmic Santa Claus.

Pray from a pure heart. If you are harboring unconfessed sin in your life, you need to confess it so you can have the boldness to enter into God's presence (PSALM 66:18).

Pray according to His will. When our desires and requests are aligned with and subjugated to the will of God, we know that He will hear and grant what we seek of Him.

Pray in His name. Jesus gave the disciples an incredible promise: "whatever you ask in My name, that I will do, that the Father may be glorified in the Son. If you ask anything in My name, I will do it" (JOHN 14:13—14). This promise is not carte blanche for every whim. If you truly pray in Jesus' name, you can pray only for that which is consistent with His perfect character and for what will bring glory to Him.

Pray with a knowledge of Scripture. We must have such a high regard for all of Scripture that we let it abide in our hearts and that we commit ourselves to knowing and obeying it. When we are controlled by His Word, we are not going to ask anything against God's will. When we want what God wants, we are guaranteed answers to our prayers.

From *Welcome to the Family*

We Should Pray Continually

[Pray] always with all prayer and supplication in the Spirit, being watchful to this end with all perseverance and supplication for all the saints.

EPHESIANS 6:18

Continue earnestly in prayer, being vigilant in it with thanksgiving.

COLOSSIANS 4:2

Watch and pray, lest you enter into temptation. The spirit indeed is willing, but the flesh is weak.

MATTHEW 26:41

The effective, fervent prayer of a righteous man avails much.

JAMES 5:16

In everything by prayer and supplication, with thanksgiving, let your requests be made known to God.

PHILIPPIANS 4:6

*F*or dedicated Christians, steadfast prayer will be as continual in their spiritual life as breathing is in their physical life. That was true of early believers and how they worshiped, both before and after the arrival of the Holy Spirit at Pentecost (ACTS 1:14; 2:42). The church first appointed deacons so the apostles could devote themselves "continually to prayer and to the ministry of the word" (ACTS 6:4). God wants believers to pray "with the spirit, and . . . with the understanding" (1 CORINTHIANS 14:15) and "without ceasing" (1 THESSALONIANS 5:17). Instead of praying to God with doubt or discontentment, the believer is to approach God in a spirit of thanksgiving. All difficulties are within God's purpose, so we can thank Him for His available power and promises.

Our greatest example of prayer comes from Jesus, who prayed frequently throughout the gospels and who still today makes continuous intercession for the growth and wellbeing of all believers (HEBREWS 7:25; ROMANS 8:34). How does Christ pray on our behalf? Surely what He prays is similar to the great high priestly prayer recorded in John 17. He prays for our security (VV. 11—12). He prays that we might be in the world but not of the world (VV. 14—15). He prays that we might be kept from evil (V. 15). He prays for our sanctification (V. 17). He prays that we will be one with Him, one with the Father, and one with one another (VV. 21—23).

From *Truth for Today* and *The God Who Loves*

We Should Nurture Our Families in Faith

These words which I command you today shall be in your heart.
You shall teach them diligently to your children, and shall talk
of them when you sit in your house, when you walk by the way,
when you lie down, and when you rise up.

DEUTERONOMY 6:6–7

He who loves father or mother more than Me is not worthy of
Me. And he who loves son or daughter more than Me is not
worthy of Me.

MATTHEW 10:37

Wives, submit to your own husbands, as is fitting in the Lord.
Husbands, love your wives and do not be bitter toward them.
Children, obey your parents in all things, for this is well pleasing
to the Lord. Fathers, do not provoke your children, lest they
become discouraged.

COLOSSIANS 3:18–21

Behold, children are a heritage from the LORD,
The fruit of the womb is a reward.
Like arrows in the hand of a warrior,
So are the children of one's youth.
Happy is the man who has his quiver full of them;
They shall not be ashamed,
But shall speak with their enemies in the gate.

PSALM 127:3–5

Our only hope to make our families everything God intended them to be comes if we first acknowledge our need for Christ and trust Him as Lord and Savior. Christ must be first in our hearts, and He demands to be first in the family. It's only when we love Him more than family that we can really love our families in the highest, purest sense. Obviously, some non-Christian families appear to be successful, but such a family has no spiritual stability.

Christian parents need to apply and obey the simple principles that are clearly set forth for them in God's Word, such as these: Constantly teach your kids the truth of God's Word (DEUTERONOMY 6:7). Discipline children when they do wrong (PROVERBS 23:13–14). And don't provoke them to anger (COLOSSIANS 3:21). Also, always keep in mind these four oft-neglected biblical principles that should lay the foundation for the Christian parent's perspective:

1. Children should be seen as a blessing, not a hardship.
2. Parenting is supposed to be a joy, not a burden.
3. Success in parenting is measured by what the parents do, not by what the child does.
4. A child's most important influences come from parents, not peers.

From *The Fulfilled Family* and *Successful Christian Parenting*

We All Have Spiritual Gifts

There are diversities of gifts, but the same Spirit. . . . The manifestation of the Spirit is given to each one for the profit of all: for to one is given the word of wisdom through the Spirit, to another the word of knowledge through the same Spirit, to another faith by the same Spirit, to another gifts of healings by the same Spirit, to another the working of miracles, to another prophecy, to another discerning of spirits, to another different kinds of tongues, to another the interpretation of tongues. But one and the same Spirit works all these things, distributing to each one individually as He wills.

1 CORINTHIANS 12:4, 7—11

Pursue love, and desire spiritual gifts, but especially that you may prophesy.

1 CORINTHIANS 14:1

Having then gifts differing according to the grace that is given to us, let us use them: if prophecy, let us prophesy in proportion to our faith; or ministry, let us use it in our ministering; he who teaches, in teaching; he who exhorts, in exhortation; he who gives, with liberality; he who leads, with diligence; he who shows mercy, with cheerfulness.

ROMANS 12:6—8

*E*ach Christian is gifted uniquely by God to help meet the needs of fellow believers in the Body. If we can recover that simple truth and live it out with new enthusiasm in our fellowships, we can restore health to the Body and at the same time fill even the deepest needs of the most troubled lives.

Spiritual gifts are offered in infinite variety, each with a different design, like snowflakes. The gifts listed in the New Testament (ROMANS 12: 1 CORINTHIANS 12) are simply categories. An individual's spiritual gift should comprise several features of the various abilities named as gifts in these passages. In other words, someone whose primary gift is teaching will probably also be gifted to some degree in wisdom, discernment, or mercy. That person's gift is a singular blend of abilities and characteristics that enable him or her to minister according to God's calling.

When we serve other Christians we serve the Lord (MATTHEW 25:40), and unselfish service is a key to personal relationships (MATTHEW 20:28—28). As followers of Christ, we must discover, develop, and deploy our spiritual gifts in service to others.

From *Introduction to Biblical Counseling*

We Should Study God's Word

[Christians in Berea] received the word with all readiness, and searched the Scriptures daily.

ACTS 17:11

We will give ourselves continually to prayer and to the ministry of the word.

ACTS 6:4

How can a young man cleanse his way?
By taking heed according to Your word.
With my whole heart I have sought You;
Oh, let me not wander from Your commandments!
Your word I have hidden in my heart,
That I might not sin against You.
Blessed are You, O LORD!
Teach me Your statutes.

PSALM 119:9—12

*T*o know God—really know Him—so that He actually speaks to us through His biblical message takes regular, effective Bible study, which requires at least five things: new birth, real desire, constant diligence, practical holiness, and prayer.

New birth, being born again, is vital. In order to get anything out of God's Word, you have to belong to God and have the guidance of the Holy Spirit (1 CORINTHIANS 2:14).

Real desire to know the Word is crucial. You need a passion for knowing God through His Word.

Constant diligence results from real desire. Bible study takes discipline. The Spirit works through the Word, and you have to work to get His message. If there is no perspiration, there will be no inspiration.

Practical holiness simply means cleaning up your life before expecting deeper insights into the Word (1 PETER 2:1–2).

Prayer is seeking the divine Source of understanding—God Himself. Scripture study and prayer were the early apostles' two top priorities (ACTS 6:4). No Christian should ever look down at the Word without first looking up at the very Source of that Word and asking for guidance. To engage in Bible study without prayer is presumption, if not sacrilege.

From *Unleashing God's Word in Your Life*

We Should Know Sound Doctrine

Test all things; hold fast what is good.

1 THESSALONIANS 5:21

Hold fast the pattern of sound words which you have heard from me, in faith and love which are in Christ Jesus.

2 TIMOTHY 1:13

All Scripture is given by inspiration of God, and is profitable for doctrine, for reproof, for correction, for instruction in righteousness.

2 TIMOTHY 3:16

If you instruct the brethren in these things, you will be a good minister of Jesus Christ, nourished in the words of faith and of the good doctrine which you have carefully followed.

1 TIMOTHY 4:6

I declare to you the gospel which I preached to you, which also you received and in which you stand, by which also you are saved, if you hold fast that word which I preached to you—unless you believed in vain. For I delivered to you first of all that which I also received: that Christ died for our sins according to the Scriptures, and that He was buried, and that He rose again the third day according to the Scriptures.

1 CORINTHIANS 15:1–4

Genuine spiritual maturity is always grounded in sound doctrine. Growth in righteousness and godly living are based on spiritual principles that must be known before they can do us any good. All spiritual growth is based on knowledge of truth. Sound doctrine is crucial to a successful spiritual walk (TITUS 2:1–15). The entire Christian life is established on knowledge of divine principles, sound doctrine, and biblical truth.

Doctrine is not the exclusive domain of seminary professors. All true Christians must be concerned with understanding sound doctrine. It is the discipline of discerning and digesting what God is saying to us in His Word so we can live lives that glorify Him. Doctrine forms the belief system that controls and compels behavior. What could be more practical—or more important? God's truth is revealed in His Word, and it is there we must ultimately go to settle any doctrinal issue.

From *The Vanishing Conscience* and
The Gospel According to the Apostles

We Should Practice Discernment

Behold, I send you out as sheep in the midst of wolves. Therefore be wise as serpents and harmless as doves.

MATTHEW 10:16

Test all things; hold fast what is good. Abstain from every form of evil.

1 THESSALONIANS 5:21–22

Beloved, do not believe every spirit, but test the spirits, whether they are of God; because many false prophets have gone out into the world.

1 JOHN 4:1

Beware lest you also fall from your own steadfastness, being led away with the error of the wicked; but grow in the grace and knowledge of our Lord and Savior Jesus Christ.

2 PETER 3:17–18

*D*iscernment—the ability to think biblically about all areas of life—is indispensable to an uncompromising life. It is incumbent upon the Christian to seize upon the discernment that God has provided for in His precious truth! Without it, Christians are at risk of being "tossed here and there by waves, and carried about by every wind of doctrine" (EPHESIANS 4:14 NASB).

Every Christian is required to be discerning, but unfortunately, discernment is an area where most Christians stumble. They exhibit little ability to measure the things they are taught against the infallible standard of God's Word, and they unwittingly engage in all kinds of unbiblical decision–making and behavior. In short, they are not armed to take a decidedly biblical stand against the onslaught of unbiblical thinking and attitudes that face them throughout their day.

Discernment intersects the Christian life at every point. And God's Word provides us with the needed discernment about every issue of life. According to Peter, God "has granted to us everything pertaining to life and godliness, through the true knowledge of Him who called us by His own glory and excellence" (2 PETER 1:3 NASB). You see, it is through the "true knowledge of Him," that we have been given everything we need to live a Christian life in this fallen world.

From *www.gty.org*

We Should Share the Good News of Jesus

This gospel of the kingdom will be preached in all the world as a witness to all the nations, and then the end will come.

MATTHEW 24:14

I am not ashamed of the gospel of Christ, for it is the power of God to salvation for everyone who believes, for the Jew first and also for the Greek. For in it the righteousness of God is revealed from faith to faith; as it is written, "The just shall live by faith."

ROMANS 1:16–17

God was in Christ reconciling the world to Himself, not imputing their trespasses to them, and has committed to us the word of reconciliation.

2 CORINTHIANS 5:19

For this reason we also thank God without ceasing, because when you received the word of God which you heard from us, you welcomed it not as the word of men, but as it is in truth, the word of God, which also effectively works in you who believe.

1 THESSALONIANS 2:13

$\mathcal{G}$ospel means "good news." What makes it truly good news is not just that heaven is free, but that sin has been conquered by God's Son.

Sadly, it has become stylish to present the gospel as something other than a remedy for sin. "Salvation" is offered as an escape from punishment, God's plan for a wonderful life, a means of fulfillment, an answer to life's problems, and a promise of free forgiveness. All those things are true, but they are byproducts of redemption, not the main issue. When sin is left unaddressed, such promises of divine blessings cheapen the message.

The gospel is good news about who Christ is and what He has done for sinners. "He made Him who knew no sin to be sin on our behalf, so that we might become the righteousness of God in Him" (2 CORINTHIANS 5:21 NASB).

"Let the wicked forsake his way, and the unrighteous man his thoughts; and let him return to the LORD, and He will have compassion on him; and to our God, for He will abundantly pardon" (ISAIAH 55:7 NASB). "If you confess with your mouth Jesus as Lord, and believe in your heart that God raised Him from the dead, you shall be saved" (ROMANS 10:9 NASB).

From *The Gospel According to the Apostles*

We Should Teach Our Children the Gospel

These words which I command you today shall be in your heart.
You shall teach them diligently to your children, and shall talk
of them when you sit in your house, when you walk by the way,
when you lie down, and when you rise up.

DEUTERONOMY 6:6–7

Train up a child in the way he should go,
And when he is old he will not depart from it.

PROVERBS 22:6

Do not provoke your children to wrath, but bring them up in
the training and admonition of the Lord.

EPHESIANS 6:4

From childhood you have known the Holy Scriptures, which
are able to make you wise for salvation through faith which is
in Christ Jesus.

2 TIMOTHY 3:15

I have no greater joy than to hear that my children walk in truth.

3 JOHN 4

*F*rom childhood most of us have heard that God loves us. The Bible tells us that love is at the very heart of who God is (1 JOHN 4:8, 16) and He is "the God of love and peace" (2 CORINTHIANS 13:11). Those wonderful truths are always among the first things we teach our children about God. And that is as it should be.

But when Scripture talks about teaching children spiritual truth, the emphasis is on thoroughness. Don't soften the parts of the message that sound unpleasant. Christ's blood, the cross, and atonement for our sins are at the heart of the message. Don't tone down the demand for surrender to Christ's lordship. Any child who is old enough to understand the basic gospel is also able by God's grace to trust Him and respond with pure surrender (MATTHEW 18:2–4).

Teach children the gospel—all of it—but understand that you may be planting the seeds for a harvest that may not be mature for many years. Children cannot be saved before they are mature enough to understand good and evil, sin and punishment, and repentance and faith. Because children mature at different times, we must teach our children patiently, consistently, faithfully over all their developing years. Encourage every step of faith as they grow.

From *The Gospel According to the Apostles* and *The God Who Loves*

Believers Can Expect Persecution

All who desire to live godly in Christ Jesus will suffer persecution.

2 TIMOTHY 3:12

Rejoice to the extent that you partake of Christ's sufferings, that when His glory is revealed, you may also be glad with exceeding joy. If you are reproached for the name of Christ, blessed are you, for the Spirit of glory and of God rests upon you. On their part He is blasphemed, but on your part He is glorified. But let none of you suffer as a murderer, a thief, an evildoer, or as a busybody in other people's matters. Yet if anyone suffers as a Christian, let him not be ashamed, but let him glorify God in this matter. . . . Therefore let those who suffer according to the will of God commit their souls to Him in doing good, as to a faithful Creator.

1 PETER 4:13–16, 19

Blessed are those who are persecuted for righteousness' sake, For theirs is the kingdom of heaven.
Blessed are you when they revile and persecute you, and say all kinds of evil against you falsely for My sake. Rejoice and be exceedingly glad, for great is your reward in heaven, for so they persecuted the prophets who were before you.

MATTHEW 5:10–12

We are hard-pressed on every side, yet not crushed; we are perplexed, but not in despair; persecuted, but not forsaken; struck down, but not destroyed.

2 CORINTHIANS 4:8–9

*T*he New Testament is filled with references to persecution, and 1 Peter in particular teaches believers how to live victoriously in the midst of hostility: 1) without losing hope; 2) without becoming bitter; 3) while trusting in their Lord; and 4) while looking for His second coming. Peter wished to impress on his readers that by living an obedient, victorious life under duress, a Christian can actually evangelize his or her hostile world (1:14; 2:1, 12, 15; 3:1–6, 13–17; 4:2; 5:8–9).

The Christian life can be summarized as a call to victory and glory through the path of suffering. Christians should deal with animosity by focusing on Jesus Christ as the model of one who maintained a triumphant attitude in the midst of hostility. First Peter 4:12–19 presents the four attitudes necessary for triumphal living in the midst of suffering:

1. Christians should expect persecution and not be surprised by it (v. 12);
2. Christians should rejoice amid difficulty (vv. 13–14);
3. Christians ought always to evaluate the cause of suffering by asking whether the suffering is self-induced or somehow due to their own ignoble actions (vv. 15–18);
4. Christians should entrust their hard times and their lives to God (v. 19).

From *MacArthur Bible Studies: 1 & 2 Peter*

Heaven Gives Us Encouragement for Life

Blessed be the God and Father of our Lord Jesus Christ, who according to His abundant mercy has begotten us again to a living hope through the resurrection of Jesus Christ from the dead, to an inheritance incorruptible and undefiled and that does not fade away, reserved in heaven for you, who are kept by the power of God through faith for salvation ready to be revealed in the last time.

1 PETER 1:3—5

You are a chosen generation, a royal priesthood, a holy nation, His own special people, that you may proclaim the praises of Him who called you out of darkness into His marvelous light.

1 PETER 2:9

Our citizenship is in heaven, from which we also eagerly wait for the Savior, the Lord Jesus Christ, who will transform our lowly body that it may be conformed to His glorious body, according to the working by which He is able even to subdue all things to Himself.

PHILIPPIANS 3:20—21

I am continually with You;
You hold me by my right hand.
You will guide me with Your counsel,
And afterward receive me to glory.

PSALM 73:23—24

*F*ocusing on heaven is an important key to experiencing joy amid trials. The richness of our inheritance should motivate us to bless God continually. We're aliens and strangers in this world (1 PETER 1:1), but we're citizens of heaven and recipients of immeasurable blessings in Christ.

Heavenly minded patience includes looking forward to our eternal inheritance and adoring God for it despite our temporal circumstances. Peter illustrated that principle in his first epistle, which was written to teach us how to live out our faith amid seemingly unbearable trials and persecutions. The Emperor Nero had accused the Christians of burning Rome, and the resulting persecution was spreading even as far as Asia Minor, where the recipients of 1 Peter lived.

We are God's "own special people," (1 PETER 2:9). As such we are at odds with Satan's evil world system and will incur its wrath. Therefore we shouldn't be surprised or intimidated by threats of persecution. That's our calling. In the tough times—which will come—we would do well to hold that assurance and remember to praise God (1 PETER 1:3—5). Bowing in praise is far better than bowing to pressure.

Praising God for our eternal inheritance should be the constant expression of our hearts, no matter what the temporal situation might be.

From *Our Sufficiency in Christ*

In the End, Unbelievers Will Go to Hell

The wicked shall be turned into hell,
And all the nations that forget God.

PSALM 9:17

The way of life winds upward for the wise,
That he may turn away from hell below.

PROVERBS 15:24

Do not fear those who kill the body but cannot kill the soul. But rather fear Him who is able to destroy both soul and body in hell.

MATTHEW 10:28

The angels will come forth, separate the wicked from among the just, and cast them into the furnace of fire. There will be wailing and gnashing of teeth.

MATTHEW 13:49—50

The cowardly, unbelieving, abominable, murderers, sexually immoral, sorcerers, idolaters, and all liars shall have their part in the lake which burns with fire and brimstone, which is the second death.

REVELATION 21:8

*B*ecause we were born in sin we were born to death, "for the wages of sin is death" (ROMANS 6:23). People do not become spiritually dead because they sin; they are sinners "by nature" and therefore born without spiritual life. Because we were dead to God, we were dead to truth, righteousness, peace, happiness, and every other good thing, no more able to respond to God than a cadaver.

Unregenerate sinners have no life by which they can respond to spiritual stimuli. No amount of love, beseeching, or spiritual truth can summon a response. People apart from God are the ungrateful dead, spiritual zombies, death-walkers, unable even to understand the gravity of their situation. They are lifeless. They may go through the motions of life, but they do not possess it. They are dead even while they live (1 TIMOTHY 5:6).

The unsaved are "by nature children of wrath" (EPHESIANS 2:3). People are not "all God's children," as some are fond of saying. Those who have not received salvation through Jesus Christ are God's enemies (ROMANS 5:10; 8:7; JAMES 4:4), not only "sons of disobedience" but consequently "children of wrath"—objects of God's eternal condemnation.

From *The Gospel According to the Apostles*

In the End, Believers Will Go to Heaven

Set your mind on things above, not on things on the earth. For you died, and your life is hidden with Christ in God. When Christ who is our life appears, then you also will appear with Him in glory.

COLOSSIANS 3:2—4

Blessed be the God and Father of our Lord Jesus Christ, who according to His abundant mercy has begotten us again to a living hope through the resurrection of Jesus Christ from the dead, to an inheritance incorruptible and undefiled and that does not fade away, reserved in heaven for you, who are kept by the power of God through faith for salvation ready to be revealed in the last time.

1 PETER 1:3—5

My sheep hear My voice, and I know them, and they follow Me. And I give them eternal life, and they shall never perish; neither shall anyone snatch them out of My hand.

JOHN 10:27—28

Do not lay up for yourselves treasures on earth, where moth and rust destroy and where thieves break in and steal; but lay up for yourselves treasures in heaven, where neither moth nor rust destroys and where thieves do not break in and steal. For where your treasure is, there your heart will be also.

MATTHEW 6:19—21

The apostle Paul was preoccupied with heaven; he knew few earthly comforts. He was beaten, stoned, left for dead, deprived of necessities, and frequently disappointed by people. But he had no concern for pleasant feelings: he wanted only to live a productive life in pursuit of his heavenly goal. We must have the same focus if we are going to pursue our heavenly reward. Christ is from heaven and in heaven. Heaven is His place, and because we are His, heaven is our place as well. If we are preoccupied with being like Him, we will naturally be preoccupied with heaven. What happens there should be more important to us than what happens here.

In the contemporary church, the increasing emphasis on success, prosperity, and personal problem-solving reflects our earthbound perspective. It's often hard for us to comprehend a future heavenly reward when, in this materialistic age, we rarely experience delayed gratification. It's easy to lose interest in heaven when we are preoccupied with this world and with prospering in this life. But to pursue Christ with the same passion as Paul, we must focus on the world to come. Heaven is our true home, and we should long to be there.

From *Truth for Today*

The law of the LORD is perfect,
    converting the soul;
The testimony of the LORD is sure,
    making wise the simple;
The statutes of the LORD are right,
    rejoicing the heart;
The commandment of the LORD is pure,
    enlightening the eyes;
The fear of the LORD is clean, enduring forever;
The judgments of the LORD are true
    and righteous altogether.
More to be desired are they than gold,
    Yea, than much fine gold;
Sweeter also than honey and the honeycomb.
Moreover by them Your servant is warned,
And in keeping them there is great reward.

PSALM 19:7–11

CONCLUSION

Scriptures to Live By

Christianity would be much easier to sell if only it had a good dose of twenty-first century inclusivism. On one level, the message of the Bible sounds so attractive and comforting: God is love! Jesus forgives your sins! That's terrific. The same gospel that tells us those things, though, also tells us to worship Jesus as Lord, that we can't earn our way to heaven, and that the only way to eternal life is through Christ. If you don't believe the gospel, you don't know God. If you don't know God, you're going to be judged without regard for your human morality.

You can't go to heaven unless you know how, and you can't know how except by reading the Bible. That's the only place where men wrote down words the Holy Spirit inspired. All Scripture is given by inspiration of God. Peter described the process: "holy men of God spoke as they were moved by the Holy Spirit" (2 PETER 1:21).

God calls all Christians to proclaim the message of Christ. Most do it by word and deed, as a part of daily living. Some make evangelism their life's work, as God called me to do. I learned early on that I can't save everybody. All I can do is proclaim the gospel. I'm not responsible for who gets saved, and neither are you. God has that responsibility, not us.

Therefore I can look over the multitude and say, as Jesus said, "Most of you won't believe." But some will believe, brought to faith through reading the Bible, talking with a friend, or hearing a preacher on the street. Then, instead of being unbelievable and foolish, these gospel words that are so hard to believe become the only balm that soothes a sinful heart; the only guide through the narrow gate that leads to eternal life; the only truth rich, complete, and holy enough to save a soul from eternal fire.

Those hard words become precious and welcome and treasured. "All that the Father gives to Christ, they will come."

They will come. Our calling is to reach them with the truth.

From *Hard to Believe*

Acknowledgments

Text in *Scriptures to Live By* was derived from the following resources written or edited by Dr. John MacArthur and published by Thomas Nelson, Inc.

The Battle for the Beginning (2001)
God in the Manger (2001)
The God Who Loves (1996)
The Gospel According to the Apostles (1993)
Hard to Believe (2003)
Introduction to Biblical Counseling (1994)
Lord, Teach Me to Pray (2003)
The MacArthur Bible Studies: Hebrews (2001)
The MacArthur Bible Studies: 1 & 2 Peter (2000)
The MacArthur Quick Reference Guide to the Bible (2001)
The MacArthur Study Bible (1997)
The Murder of Jesus (2000).
Our Sufficiency in Christ (1991)
Rediscovering Expository Preaching (1992)
Rediscovering Pastoral Ministry (1995)
Successful Christian Parenting (1998)
Truth for Today (2001)
Twelve Ordinary Men (2002)
Unleashing God's Word in Your Life (2003)
The Vanishing Conscience (1994)
Welcome to the Family (2004)

For More Information

JOHN MACARTHUR, one of today's foremost Bible teachers, is the author of numerous bestselling books that have touched millions of lives. He is pastor-teacher of Grace Community Church in Sun Valley, California, and president of The Master's College and Seminary. He is also president of Grace to You, the ministry that produces the internationally syndicated radio program Grace to You and a host of print, audio, and Internet resources—all featuring John's popular verse-by-verse teaching. He also authored the notes in *The MacArthur Study Bible,* which has been awarded the Gold Medallion and has sold more than 1 million copies. John and his wife, Patricia, have four children (all married), who have given them fourteen grandchildren.

For more information about John MacArthur and his Bible-teaching resources, contact Grace to You at:

800-55-GRACE (800-554-7223)

or *www.gty.org*